How to MAKE FOOD your KIDS WILL ACTUALLY EAT

Anouska Emily Mauree is a Mauritian-British mum of two who loves making mealtimes fun. With a background in childcare, she has always loved helping kids find the fun in food but she got into her channel in earnest in lockdown when she started to grow a following for her brilliantly simple food hacks. She has gone viral for food that is both fun and delicious, such as her viral smashed crispy parmesan broccoli, taco cups, Disney Bluey toast and twisted egg and soldiers. She has worked with brands such as Tesco, Lidl, Nestle, M&S, OXO, Deli Kitchen, Ninja Kitchen and been a judge at The Quality Food Awards 2024 and 2025.

@emilyscooking_

@emilyscooking_

How to MAKE FOOD your KIDS WILL ACTUALLY EAT

Over 100 snacktivities, lunchboxes and food hacks

Anouska Emily Mauree

hamlyn

For my boys, Shafi and Kai

hamlyn

First published in Great Britain in
2026 by Hamlyn, an imprint of
Octopus Publishing Group Ltd
Carmelite House
50 Victoria Embankment
London EC4Y 0DZ
www.octopusbooks.co.uk

An Hachette UK Company
www.hachette.co.uk

The authorized representative in the
EEA is Hachette Ireland, 8 Castlecourt
Centre, Dublin 15, D15 XTP3, Ireland
(email: info@hbgi.ie)

Distributed in the US by
Hachette Book Group
1290 Avenue of the Americas,
4th and 5th Floors,
New York, NY 10104

Distributed in Canada by
Canadian Manda Group,
664 Annette Street, Toronto, Ontario,
Canada M6S 2C8

ISBN: 978-0-60063-960-2
eISBN: 978-0-60063-961-9

A CIP catalogue record for this book
is available from the British Library.

Printed and bound in China.

10 9 8 7 6 5 4 3 2 1

Photography by Anouska
Emily Mauree

Photography on pages 7, 8, 32, 37
(top centre), 60, 80 and 164 by
Jamie Orlando Smith

Publisher: Kate Fox
Senior Developmental Editor:
    Pauline Bache
Art Director: Jaz Bahra
Illustrator: Tom Widdrington
Copyeditor: Joanna Smith
Assistant Production Managers:
    Nic Jones and Lucy Carter

All electric oven temperatures are
for fan-assisted ovens. To adapt for
a conventional oven, increase the
oven temperature by 20°C. Air fryer
cooking times and temperatures
can vary, so always check during
cooking if needed.

CONTENTS

INTRODUCTION

Hey, I'm Anouska, also known as Emily (@emilyscooking_). If you've picked up this book, I'm glad I've got your attention. Once you flick through the pages, you'll see this isn't your typical mummy cookbook. Instead you'll find a collection of fun, spontaneous, refreshingly unique and wholesome recipes.

As a mum of two boys (Shafi and Kai), I've learned that meal times aren't just about feeding the family, they're about bringing everyone together. With a background in education and a passion for cooking, I approach food prep as a fun, hands-on experience. I believe that when kids get involved in the kitchen, they're not only learning valuable life skills, they're more likely to appreciate what's on their plate, too.

I started sharing my recipe ideas on Instagram and they were a huge hit. I couldn't believe the response I received, but it encouraged me to continue to share ideas for people of all ages, especially the little ones. There's nothing better than seeing other families recreate the recipes my boys and I make at home. Cooking with children doesn't have to be a hassle, it can be a chance to get creative and a family bonding adventure. I know there are times when the kitchen feels more like a battlefield than a fun zone, but with a little planning and imagination, I've figured out ways to keep it light-hearted. Whether it's letting the children mix ingredients, assemble veg into characters, or choose their own toppings, I've discovered that the more interactive the process, the more they're excited to eat.

I've shared some of my favourite tips to get little ones involved, while keeping chaos to a minimum. From simple tasks that build their confidence in the kitchen, to fun challenges that make them feel like mini chefs, these ideas will make cooking feel less like a chore and more like a shared adventure.

The book includes some hearty recipes, perfect for family meals, and plenty of cool hacks along the way. Together, we'll make every meal an opportunity for laughter, learning and, of course, delicious food. Roll up your sleeves, and let's get cooking!

HELPFUL HINTS

As you embark on these recipes, keep the following important hints in mind:

Child-Friendly Tasks Each recipe includes something your child can help with – from stirring to arranging ingredients, there's no shortage of fun activities for little hands to enjoy! Cooking is a great way to bond, learn and make lasting memories with your family.

Safety First Always supervise your children when cooking, especially around sharp equipment and hot surfaces like the oven, stove and air fryer. The kitchen can be a dangerous place, but with guidance, kids can safely assist in meal preparation.

Air Fryer Caution If you're using baking paper in the air fryer, make sure it's only a small piece that fits under the food. A large piece can fly up and catch fire – please be mindful.

Adjust to Suit Your Taste Every recipe is a guideline, so feel free to adjust herbs, spices, salt and pepper to suit your family's preferences. Cooking is all about experimenting and finding out what tastes best to you.

Calories Don't Matter Here You won't find calorie counts in this book because, honestly, that's not what cooking with kids is all about. It's about having fun, eating together and enjoying the process of creating something delicious.

Love, Anoushka Emily x

BREAKFAST

This chapter is all about the breakfast recipes I've created. Some are classics that took over the internet, others are fresh new twists I've made to keep things interesting – all are guaranteed to spice up your morning routine. Whether you're looking for something quick and easy midweek or a weekend breakfast project, there's a little something here for every kind of morning. So shake up your breakfast game and start the day off right with something banging for you and your family.

EGGS IN A BOAT

This one takes the 'egg in a hole' recipe to a whole new level. Over 12 million people liked this on Instagram, and it's perfect for tearing and sharing with family and friends. You can make as many holes as you like, depending on the size of your baguette, or try individual portions using small baguettes or bread rolls.

Make sure the bread is soft and fresh so it doesn't get overcooked during baking.

Those bits of bread you cut out to make the holes are amazing for breaking the egg yolks and scooping them up.

SERVES 3

—

1 baguette

2–3 tablespoons olive oil or melted butter

1–2 teaspoons filling per hole – I used chilli oil, Green Sauce (see page 167) and Red Sauce (see page 166)

3 eggs

grated Parmesan cheese (optional)

pinch each of paprika, dried mixed herbs and garlic granules

salt and pepper

1 Preheat the oven to 180°C (400°F), Gas Mark 6. Place the baguette on a lined baking tray and use a sharp knife to cut holes a little bit bigger than your eggs.

2 Place the offcuts of bread on the tray. Drizzle the olive oil or melted butter all over the bread and in the holes.

3 Spoon the fillings into the holes, using the same one in each, or a mixture of different fillings.

4 Carefully crack an egg into each hole.

5 Sprinkle Parmesan over the top (if using) and finish with a sprinkle of paprika, mixed herbs, garlic granules and salt and pepper. Bake for 15–20 minutes, depending on how you like your eggs cooked, checking from time to time towards the end of cooking. Slice and enjoy.

TWISTED EGGY TOAST & SOLDIERS

This is a unique version of the classic egg and soldiers and you don't even need to boil your eggs. I bake the cut-off crusts alongside as a crispy treat to dip in the yolk.

SERVES 1
—
1 slice of bread
butter, for spreading
1 egg
pinch of chilli flakes
    (optional)
salt and pepper

1 Preheat the air fryer to 180°C, or the oven to 180°C (400°F), Gas Mark 6. Cut the crusts off the bread. Spread butter over the bread and the separated crusts.

2 Use a sharp knife to cut the corners of the bread at an angle, leaving the widest part of each wedge attached to the slice.

3 Take one cut point and tuck it into the cut on the adjacent edge. Continue with all 4 edges to form a basket, then use a spoon or your fingertips to flatten the middle of the basket.

4 Carefully crack the egg into the basket. Season with chilli flakes, if using, and a pinch of salt and pepper. Use a spatula to transfer the bread basket to the air fryer or onto a baking tray in the oven and arrange the crusts around it.

5 Cook for 7–10 minutes in the air fryer or 8–15 minutes in the oven for a runny yolk, checking after about 4 minutes when you remove the cooked crusts. If you're using a large egg or prefer the yolk well done, add 2–3 minutes to the cooking time.

EASY CHEESY BACON TOAST

Bacon, cheese and toast is a common breakfast or lunch for many of us, but have you made it like this before? It's banging, trust me!

Cut thin slices of cheese from your favourite cheese blocks at home – mild Cheddar, mature Cheddar and Red Leicester all work well.

MAKES 6

—

2 slices of bread
6 slices of cheese
6 rashers of bacon

1 Preheat the air fryer to 185°C, or the oven to 200°C (425°F), Gas Mark 7. Cut each slice of bread into three and place a slice of cheese on each piece.

2 Wrap a rasher of bacon around each piece of bread, completely enclosing the cheese.

3 Add the toast pieces to the air fryer or onto a baking tray lined with baking paper if cooking in the oven.

4 Cook in the air fryer or oven for 10–15 minutes, until the bacon is cooked to your liking.

THREE-INGREDIENT PAINS AU CHOCOLATE

A cheaty way of making delicious pains au chocolate at home, this affordable version allows you to create a classic pastry in minutes. As well as making a tasty and simple breakfast, this is a great idea for cake sales and coffee mornings at school.

I used Kinder bars, but other small chocolate bars or strips of squares from a larger bar of chocolate work well, too.

MAKES 8

—

325g (11½oz) ready-
   rolled puff pastry
16 small chocolate bars
1 egg, beaten

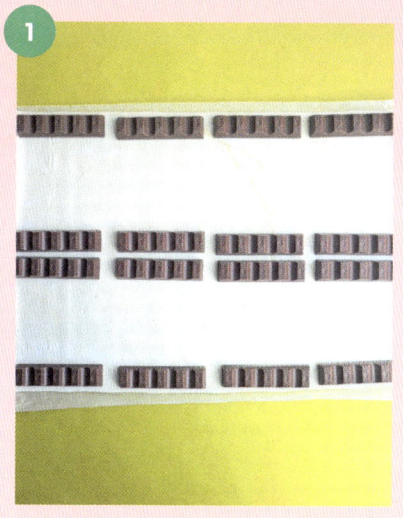

1 Preheat the oven to 200°C (425°F), Gas Mark 7. Unroll the puff pastry on its baking paper. Make a line of 4 chocolate bars at each long end of the pastry and 2 lines in the centre, leaving a little gap between them.

2 Using a sharp knife, cut the puff pastry into 8 equal rectangles with a chocolate bar at each end.

3 Fold the pastry over the chocolate bar at each end of each pastry rectangle, then stretch the pastry a little and roll both ends towards each other until they meet in the centre.

4 Place the baking paper on a baking tray and brush some of the beaten egg on the pastries.

5 Turn them over, brush again with some beaten egg and make sure they are not touching. Bake in the oven for 15–20 minutes until puffed and golden.

TOAST CHARACTERS

Back to school is never easy so this is a great way to get your little ones excited for school – by making it a celebration! All you need is toasted bread, spreads, fruit and nuts and you can create all these cute animal characters.

Here are a few of mine, but you can make your own characters, too.

Try this out for any special occasion, or just if your child needs cheering up.

BEAR

chocolate spread
3 slices of banana
3 blueberries

FISH

cream cheese
2 slices of banana (1 halved)
1 blueberry
16 slices of strawberry

CAT

peanut butter
3 slices of strawberry
6 strips of apple
2 blueberries

FOX

cream cheese
marmalade
2 slices of banana
2 slices of strawberry
3 blueberries

OWL

peanut butter
1 peanut
4 slices of banana
4 slices of strawberry
2 blueberries

BUNNY

cream cheese
½ banana, halved
2 blueberries
2 slices of strawberry (1 halved)
6 strips of apple

CHEESY EGGS IN A BAGEL

Easy to prepare and easy on the clearing up, these are my perfectly cooked sunny-side-up eggs in delicious pesto and cheese bagels. It's a popular breakfast in my family, but I also make them when friends come over for brunch, with some avocado and fried halloumi on the side. Pesto and eggs is such a good combo.

Try using my Green Sauce (see page 167) instead of ready-made pesto, or swap for butter, garlic butter or red pesto instead.

SERVES 2

—

70g (2½oz) mature
   Cheddar cheese,
   grated
1 bagel, split open
4 teaspoons pesto
2 eggs
paprika, garlic granules
   or dried oregano, for
   sprinkling
salt and pepper

1 Preheat the air fryer to 180°C, or the oven to 180°C (400°F), Gas Mark 6. Line a baking tray with baking paper. Sprinkle half the grated cheese on the tray.

2 Gently enlarge the holes in the bagel halves with your fingers a little, then spread the cut sides with 1 teaspoon of pesto on each.

3 Place the bagels on the cheese, cut sides down, then spread the remaining pesto on the tops of the bagels and sprinkle with the remaining cheese.

4 Crack the eggs onto the bagels, making sure the yolks are in the holes. Season your eggs with salt and pepper and sprinkle with paprika, garlic granules or oregano.

5 Cook for 12–18 minutes in the air fryer or 15–20 minutes in the oven, checking from time to time so your eggs are cooked to your liking. If you prefer set yolks, cook for a little longer.

STUFFED BEAN & CHEESE CRUMPETS

It's hard to beat a classic buttered crumpet but, trust me, this is a game changer – and over 18 million people agreed on Instagram! By slicing a pocket in the side of the crumpet you can add fillings as well as toppings, and the crumpets soak up all the flavours beautifully.

SERVES 1
–
1 crumpet
butter
1 tablespoon baked
   beans
2 tablespoons grated
   Cheddar cheese
pinch of dried mixed
   herbs

Get creative with the fillings and toppings. Try my Red Sauce (see page 166) inside with cheese, and sprinkle the top with paprika.

1 Preheat the air fryer to 180°C, or the oven to 180°C (400°F), Gas Mark 6. Carefully cut a slit into the side of your crumpet to make a pocket. Make sure you don't slice all the way through.

2 Spread a little butter inside.

3 Add the baked beans, taking care not to overfill or they'll leak out during cooking. Add half the grated cheese.

4 Close up the crumpet to enclose the fillings. Spread the top with a little more butter and sprinkle with the remaining cheese and some mixed herbs.

5 Cook in the air fryer or oven for 7–10 minutes, until golden. The cooking time will vary with the number of crumpets you are cooking.

CUTE CRAB CROISSANTS

These crab croissants are a cute way to start the morning. We adore them at home – without fail they always make my sons smile!

MAKES 2

—

2 croissants
chocolate spread
3 strawberries
1 banana
4 blueberries

1 Split open your croissants and spread thickly with chocolate spread. Close them again.

2 For the strawberry tongues, cut off the green stems then cut 2 slices of strawberry from top to bottom. Place the tongues in the middles of the croissants, poking out.

3 For the eyes, slice a banana into chunks and spear 4 chunks on cocktail sticks. Add a little bit of chocolate spread on top of each.

If you prefer, jam is another great filling.

The eyes are held in position with cocktail sticks.

4 Stick a blueberry onto the chocolate spread on top of each chunk of banana and poke the sticks into the croissants.

5 For the claws, cut 2 strawberries in half, then cut out a small wedge from the tip of each half. Place them next to the croissants.

SIMPLE SHAKSHUKA

Shakshuka is a vibrant and flavourful dish with roots in North African and Middle Eastern cuisine. This simple one-pot dish of poached eggs nestled in a rich, spiced tomato sauce is packed with flavour and goodness. Enjoy with crusty bread at breakfast or a fresh salad at lunch – it's the perfect choice at any time of day.

Add a tin of chickpeas or some chopped chorizo at the same time as the tomatoes for a more substantial meal.

SERVES 4

—

2 teaspoons vegetable or olive oil

1 onion, chopped

1 red chilli, deseeded and finely chopped (optional)

1 red pepper, cored, deseeded and diced

2–3 garlic cloves, sliced

1 tablespoon chopped fresh coriander

2 x 400g (14oz) cans chopped tomatoes

1 teaspoon caster sugar

1–2 tablespoons harissa paste

1–2 teaspoons paprika

1–2 teaspoons ground cumin

1 tablespoon tomato purée

4–8 eggs

salt and pepper

TO GARNISH

coriander leaves

crumbled feta cheese

chopped spring onion

chilli powder (optional)

1 Heat the oil in a frying pan with a lid over a low-medium heat, add the onion, chilli, red pepper, garlic and coriander and fry for 15 minutes or until soft.

2 Stir in the tomatoes, sugar, harissa, spices and tomato purée, season to taste, then let it bubble for 10–15 minutes until thick, adding a little water if it becomes dry.

3 Using the back of a large spoon, make a few dips in the sauce, then crack an egg into each one. Put a lid on the pan and cook over a low heat for 6–8 minutes.

4 Check the eggs are done to your liking, cooking for a little longer if necessary. Garnish with coriander leaves, feta, spring onions and a sprinkle of chilli powder, if using.

FRENCH TOAST BAGEL BITES

These are a fun twist on classic French toast – perfect for a quick breakfast, brunch treat, snack or dessert.

Choose your favourite bagels – plain or cinnamon work well.

Serve with fruit and a hot drink.

SERVES 1–2

–

1 bagel
1 large egg
1 teaspoon vanilla
   extract
¼ teaspoon ground
   cinnamon
pinch of salt
100ml (3½fl oz) milk (any
   kind)
1 tablespoon butter
icing sugar mixed with
   ground cinnamon, for
   dusting
fresh berries, to serve
   (optional)

1 Slice the bagel into bite-sized pieces.

2 In a bowl, whisk together the egg, vanilla extract, cinnamon and salt until smooth, then add the milk and whisk again until well combined.

3 Put the bagel bites into the bowl with the egg mixture and toss and turn to coat them evenly, until all the liquid has been absorbed.

4 Melt the butter in a frying pan over a medium heat. Place the coated bagel bites into the pan and cook for 2–3 minutes per side, or until they are golden brown and crispy.

5 Transfer them to a plate and dust with the icing sugar and cinnamon mixture. Serve warm with fresh berries, if liked.

3 TOASTIVITY IDEAS

Try these simple but effective ideas with your children at the weekend and on school holidays. The kids can have fun while you make a cuppa for yourself, just in time to pop the bread in the toaster!

—

EACH OPTION MAKES 1

SMILEY FACE TOAST

Press your fingertips down on a slice of bread to create a smiley face. Toast it and serve.

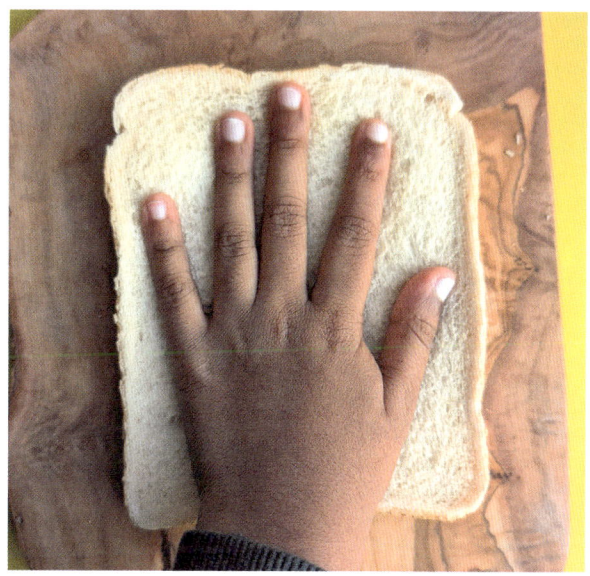

PAINTED TOAST

Use chocolate milkshake or add a few drops of food colouring to milk to make edible paints. Get some clean brushes and get creative (but try not to soak the bread too much!). Pop in the toaster and enjoy.

HANDPRINT TOAST

Press your hand down on a slice of bread to make a handprint, then toast to your liking.

LUNCH SAVERS

Lunchtime can sometimes feel like a challenge, especially when you're trying to find something that's both quick and will actually get eaten. This chapter is packed with creative lunch ideas that turn everyday ingredients into fun and tasty meals the kids will love. From sandwiches with a twist to snackable bites to keep things interesting, whether you're making packed lunches or looking for a quick at-home option, these ideas will give you and your little ones something exciting to look forward to.

SCARY MONSTER SANDWICH

This is a fun idea for your child's back-to-school packed lunch, but also perfect for Halloween, of course.

Bite your scary sandwich before it bites you!

SERVES 1–2

—

2 slices of bread
butter
1 iceberg lettuce leaf,
    halved
2 large slices of chorizo,
    salami or pepperoni
1 slice of cheese
4 slices of cucumber
4 blueberries
4 strips of red pepper

1 Cut the slices of bread in half, then spread with butter and top 2 of the pieces with lettuce.

2 Place the chorizo or salami slices on the lettuce to make tongues, letting them stick out slightly over the edge of the bread.

3 Cut the slice of cheese in half in a zigzag pattern to make 2 sets of teeth.

4 Place the teeth on top of the tongues, then pop the other pieces of bread on top to close the sandwiches.

5 Place the cucumber and blueberries in place for the eyes, then add the red pepper strips to make eyebrows.

PORTABLE PASTA STICKS

Fancy a fun food activity with the kids? Well, look no further. Transform a boring bowl of pasta into a fun and portable lunch the kids can make themselves.

Mix up the toppings, depending on what your children like. Try mushrooms, onions, pesto, peas, cooked chicken, ham or different cheeses.

MAKES 4

—

70g (2½oz) dried penne
   pasta
4–6 tablespoons Red
   Sauce (see page 166)
   or tomato sauce
70g (2½oz) mozzarella
   cheese, grated
70g (2½oz) Red Leicester
   cheese, grated
handful of sweetcorn
½ green pepper, cored,
   deseeded and diced
1 large tomato, diced
2 slices of chorizo,
   shredded

1 Preheat the oven to 180°C (400°F), Gas Mark 6. Boil the pasta according to packet instructions, drain and leave to cool. Slowly thread the penne pasta onto 4 skewers, a piece at a time.

2 Place the skewers on a baking tray lined with baking paper and spread your sauce over.

3 Mix the 2 cheeses together and sprinkle on the pasta.

4 Sprinkle over the toppings – we use sweetcorn, green pepper, tomatoes and chorizo. Everyone can choose their own and make their own skewers.

5 Cook in the oven for 20–30 minutes, or until the cheese is nice and golden and the veggies are soft.

TASTY TORTILLA TART

This tortilla tart – packed with veggies, eggs and cheese – is a unique way to serve lunch. It's so adaptable, you can add just about anything you want (think mushrooms, peppers, ham or spring onions) before you pop it in the oven to bake.

If you prefer, use mini tortillas (or cut up big ones) to make individual tarts in small tart tins or muffin tins. Everyone can layer their own ingredients.

SERVES 3–4

—

2 soft flour tortillas
100–125g (3½–4½oz) Cheddar cheese, grated
handful of baby spinach
100g (3½oz) sweetcorn
1 tomato, sliced
¼ red onion, sliced
3–4 eggs
½ teaspoon Cajun seasoning
melted butter, for brushing
salt

1 Preheat the oven to 200°C (425°F), Gas Mark 7. Place the tortillas, one on top of the other, in a medium cake tin. Sprinkle with a layer of grated cheese.

2 Layer the spinach on top, followed by the sweetcorn.

3 Now make a layer of tomato, followed by the red onion.

4 Crack the eggs into the tart, or beat them together first if you prefer. Add the remaining cheese and sprinkle with the Cajun seasoning and salt.

5 Brush the edges of the tortillas with the butter, then bake in the oven for 16–20 minutes, checking from time to time, until the eggs are done to your liking. Slice and serve.

RAINBOW PITTA PIZZAS

Get ready to create pizzas as colourful as a rainbow and as tasty as can be. This is the perfect way for kids to explore their creativity in the kitchen. With bright, fresh toppings in every colour of the rainbow, each bite is a burst of flavour and fun. It's a pizza perfection!

SERVES 2
-
3–5 tablespoons ready-made tomato and herb sauce
2 pitta breads, halved
100g (3½oz) Cheddar cheese, grated
6–8 cherry tomatoes, chopped
½ orange pepper, cored, deseeded and diced
140g (5oz) sweetcorn
½ green pepper, cored, deseeded and diced
½ small red onion, finely chopped

1 Preheat the air fryer to 180°C, or the oven to 180°C (400°F), Gas Mark 6. Spread a thin layer of tomato and herb sauce evenly over one side of each pitta half.

2 Sprinkle the cheese in an even layer over the top of the sauce.

3 Arrange some pieces of cherry tomato in a curved line around the edge of each pitta, then make a line of orange pepper inside the tomatoes.

4 Arrange lines of sweetcorn and green pepper in the same way, then finish with some red onion, to create a rainbow.

5 Cook for 6–8 minutes in the air fryer or 8–10 minutes in the oven, or until the cheese is melted and bubbling and the edges of the pittas are crispy.

BRIOCHE ROLL LOLLIES

We make these for lunches, after-school snacks, picnics and play dates. They work perfectly with sweet or savoury fillings and are a great idea for a fun and easy meal.

–

EACH OPTION MAKES 1

You will need a sandwich toaster or waffle maker for these, plus some wooden lolly sticks.

PESTO CHICKEN

1 brioche roll, split open
mayonnaise
small handful of baby spinach
1 slice of cooked chicken
1 teaspoon pesto

Open the roll and spread mayonnaise on both cut sides. Lay the spinach on one side, top with the rolled-up slice of chicken and smear the pesto over the top. Place a lolly stick at one end and close the roll over to enclose it. Cook in a sandwich toaster or waffle maker for 3–5 minutes until crispy.

PIZZA

1 brioche roll, split open
2 teaspoons Red Sauce (see page 166) or ready-made pizza sauce
handful of grated mozzarella or Cheddar cheese
3 slices of pepperoni

Open the roll and spread the sauce on both cut sides, then top with the grated cheese. Arrange the pepperoni slices on one side, place a lolly stick at one end and close the roll over to enclose it. Cook in a sandwich toaster or waffle maker for 3–5 minutes until crispy.

BANANA & PEANUT BUTTER

1 brioche roll, split open
2 tablespoons smooth peanut butter
½ banana, sliced

Open the roll and spread peanut butter on both cut sides. Arrange the banana slices on one side, place a lolly stick at one end and close the roll over to enclose it. Cook in a sandwich toaster or waffle maker for 3–5 minutes until crispy.

FRANKFURTER

1 brioche roll, split open
tomato ketchup
yellow mustard
1 cooked frankfurter, halved lengthways

Open the roll, smear ketchup over one cut side and top with a squiggle of yellow mustard. Place the halved frankfurter on the other side. Place a lolly stick at one end and close the roll over to enclose it. Cook in a sandwich toaster or waffle maker for 3–5 minutes until crispy.

OMELETTE TOAST CUPS

Enjoy my veggie-packed toast cups warm as a hearty brunch or lunch, or cold in packed lunches and picnics. I used peppers, spinach, mushrooms, onions, sweetcorn and peas for this version, but feel free to try different fillings to make them your own.

Let the toast cups cool slightly before removing them from the muffin tray.

MAKES 6

—

2 tablespoons melted
    butter or olive oil

4 large eggs

4 tablespoons milk

70–90g (2½–3¼oz)
    mixed vegetables,
    finely diced

70g (2½oz) Cheddar
    cheese, grated

1 teaspoon dried mixed
    herbs

1 teaspoon paprika

1 teaspoon garlic
    granules

6 slices of white bread

salt and pepper

1 Preheat the oven to 180°C (400°F), Gas Mark 6, and grease a 6-hole muffin tray with the butter or oil. In a jug, whisk together the eggs, milk, vegetables, half the cheese, the herbs, spices and seasoning.

2 Make a cut into all sides of the slices of bread.

3 Carefully press the bread into the holes in the muffin tray, shaping the slices into cups. Ensure you have a nice cup shape in each muffin hole.

4 Pour some of the egg mixture into the centre of each bread cup, filling them nearly to the top. Sprinkle the remaining cheese on top.

5 Bake the cups in the oven for 12–15 minutes, until the eggs are set and lightly golden on top. You can check by inserting a toothpick into the centre of an egg – if it comes out clean, they're ready.

FAKEAWAY CORN DOGS

Who loves corn dogs? I do and my boys do, too. With these,
there's no need for deep frying and they taste amazing. Such an
affordable and easy fakeaway!

MAKES 6

—

400g (14oz) pre-rolled
   pizza dough
6 frankfurters
200–250g (7–9oz)
   mozzarella or Cheddar
   cheese, grated
2 eggs, beaten
pinch of sugar
panko breadcrumbs,
   for coating
salt and pepper
sauces, to serve

1 Preheat the oven to 180°C (400°F), Gas Mark 6. Unroll the pizza dough on a work surface. Place the frankfurters on top, then cut the dough into even rectangles around them.

2 Sprinkle over plenty of cheese, then fold in the ends of the dough rectangles and use your hands to roll up the frankfurters in the dough to fully enclose them.

3 Insert a skewer halfway up through each frankfurter. Season the beaten eggs with salt, pepper and the sugar and place in a shallow bowl. Dip each corn dog into the egg, then into the breadcrumbs to coat all over.

4 Place them on a baking tray lined with baking paper and cook in the oven for about 20 minutes, until golden.

5 Serve with sauces of your choice.

CHICKEN & HIDDEN VEG NUGGETS

Nuggets: we love them and they're one of the things I one hundred per cent know that the boys will eat. I sneak some hidden veggies into them, too, so it's win-win!

SERVES 4

—

500g (1lb 2oz) minced chicken

1 courgette, grated

1 carrot, grated

1 egg

1 teaspoon paprika

1 teaspoon dried oregano

1 teaspoon ground cumin

1 teaspoon garlic granules

1 teaspoon all-purpose seasoning

4 tablespoons panko breadcrumbs, plus extra for coating

vegetable oil

salt and pepper

tomato ketchup, to serve

1 Preheat the oven to 180°C (400°F), Gas Mark 6. Place the chicken, courgette, carrot, egg, seasoning and breadcrumbs in a large bowl.

2 Use your hands to mix it all together, then divide the mixture into about 20 nuggets.

You can also shallow fry the nuggets on a low-medium heat until golden on both sides and cooked through.

Try serving them with potato wedges and My Special Salad (see page 168).

3 Fill a bowl with some extra breadcrumbs. Roll the nuggets in the breadcrumbs one at a time until coated all over.

4 Space the nuggets out on a baking tray lined with baking paper. Spray with vegetable oil.

5 Cook in the oven for 40–50 minutes, flipping them over halfway through the cooking time, until golden and cooked through. Serve with ketchup.

PUFF PASTRY TWISTS

Puff pastry twists are our go-to in the local supermarket bakery, but here's how to make them at home. You can mix this up with a number of different fillings and make them whatever size you like. I've gone for one savoury and one sweet.

MAKES 12
-
325g (11½oz) ready-
   rolled puff pastry
1 egg, beaten

SAVOURY FILLING
3–4 tablespoons Green
   Sauce (see page 167)
   or ready-made pesto
70g (2½oz) Cheddar
   cheese, grated

SWEET FILLING
3–4 tablespoons
   ready-made custard
50g (1¾oz) chocolate
   chips

1 Preheat the oven to 200°C (425°F), Gas Mark 7. Unroll the pastry and cut in half. Spread the pesto over half of one piece and sprinkle with the cheese. Repeat with the custard and chocolate.

2 Fold the bare sides of the pastry pieces over the fillings and flatten down. Cut each piece into 6 strips.

3 Twist the strips using your fingers and spread out on the paper. Brush with beaten egg and cook in the oven for 15–20 minutes, until golden and crisp.

TORTILLA PINWHEELS MAKES 4 OF EACH

Tortilla pinwheels are a fun way to interest kids in what is essentially a healthy sandwich. Customize them with your favourite fillings!

HUMMUS & SALAD

1 large soft flour tortilla
4 tablespoons Easy Hummus
   (see page 169) or ready-made
   hummus
a few salad leaves
1 small carrot, grated
½ tomato, diced

Place the tortilla on a board, spread with the hummus and top with the veggies. Roll up tightly, then slice into 2.5cm (1 inch) pinwheels.

HAM & CHEESE

1 large soft flour tortilla
butter
5 slices of ham
60g (2¼oz) Cheddar cheese,
   grated
6 slices of cucumber
mayonnaise

Place the tortilla on a board, spread with butter, top with ham, cheese and cucumber and squeeze on a little mayonnaise. Roll up tightly, then slice into 2.5cm (1 inch) pinwheels.

UPSIDE-DOWN SAUSAGE ROLLS

Baking frankfurters with buttery, flaky puff pastry on top creates a crispy, golden exterior and a soft and juicy filling. These easy-to-make treats are perfect for a quick lunch or a party appetizer, a creative take on a comfort food favourite.

Serve with sauces of your choice. I always serve mine with mustard and ketchup.

MAKES 6

—

60g (2¼oz) Parmesan
  cheese, grated
3 frankfurters, halved
  lengthways
160g (5¾oz) ready-
  rolled puff pastry
  (½ a sheet)
1 egg, beaten
1 teaspoon sesame seeds
sauces, to serve

1 Preheat the oven to 200°C (425°F), Gas Mark 7. Line a baking tray with baking paper and sprinkle the Parmesan all over it. Arrange the frankfurters, cut sides down, on the cheese, evenly spaced.

2 Unroll the puff pastry and cut into 6 long rectangles to fit neatly over the frankfurters. Lay a piece of pastry on top of each frankfurter.

3 Use the tines of a fork to press down the sides of the pastry around each frankfurter.

4 Brush them all over with beaten egg, then sprinkle with the sesame seeds.

5 Bake in the oven for 15–20 minutes until puffed and golden.

TOMATO FLOWER TARTS

Your kids will love creating their own cute flower tarts. This one is definitely a crowd pleaser – the boys and I made these for a gathering with friends and they were gone within minutes!

MAKES 8

—

olive oil, for drizzling

½ teaspoon dried thyme

½ teaspoon dried oregano

½ teaspoon paprika

½ teaspoon garlic granules

4 yellow cherry tomatoes, halved

24 red cherry tomatoes, halved

85g (3oz) Parmesan cheese, grated

325g (11½oz) ready-rolled puff pastry

1 egg, beaten

salt and pepper

a few basil leaves, to garnish

Garnish with basil leaves to enhance the flower theme!

1 Preheat the oven to 200°C (425°F), Gas Mark 7. Lay 2 sheets of baking paper on the work surface. Drizzle 4 little patches of oil onto each sheet of paper and sprinkle over the herbs and spices.

2 Get creative and arrange the cherry tomatoes, cut sides down, into flower shapes on top of the patches of oil.

3 Sprinkle the Parmesan on top of the tomatoes.

4 Unroll the puff pastry and cut out 8 discs, using a saucer or bowl as a guide, a little larger than the flowers. Place the pastry over the tomatoes and use the tines of a fork to press down the edges and make a few holes in the tops.

5 Brush the pastry with beaten egg, transfer the tarts on their paper to 2 baking trays and cook in the oven for about 15 minutes, until golden. Carefully flip the tarts over using a spatula and add basil leaves for that extra touch!

FILLED MINI TACO CONES

These neat little cones will add an interesting twist to your meal. They're great for picky eaters, as children love filling the cones with hummus and veggie sticks.

MAKES 4

-

2 mini soft flour tortillas
vegetable oil

TO SERVE
Easy Hummus (see page 169)
1 tomato, sliced
cucumber, carrot and pepper batons

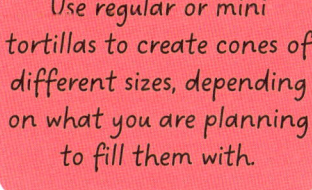

Use regular or mini tortillas to create cones of different sizes, depending on what you are planning to fill them with.

You will need toothpicks to hold the cones together while they cook.

1 Preheat the air fryer to 180°C, or the oven to 180°C (400°F), Gas Mark 6. Cut your tortillas neatly in half.

2 Make the cones by rolling up the tortillas, with the point forming in the centre of the straight edge.

3 Use toothpicks to hold the shape of the cones. Spray all over with a little bit of vegetable oil.

4 Cook for 4–8 minutes in the air fryer or 6–8 minutes in the oven, until golden. Remove the sticks, add your fillings and enjoy!

CUCUMBER SUSHI BOATS

Here's a fresh and fun twist on sushi! We have made these so many times and they're always a big hit on play dates and picnics. Serve with a side of soy sauce, chilli oil or pickles if you like.

If your child isn't keen on tuna, use chopped cooked chicken or ham instead.

MAKES 12–14

-

125g (4½oz) can tuna, drained

90g (3¼oz) sweetcorn

2–3 tablespoons mayonnaise

1 cucumber

300g (10½oz) cooked and cooled jasmine rice

SEASONING

black and white sesame seeds

paprika

garlic granules

sesame oil

onion powder

salt and pepper

1 Mix the seasoning ingredients together in a small bowl, according to your taste. Mix the tuna, sweetcorn and mayonnaise in another bowl, then add some of the seasoning and mix well.

2 Cut the cucumber in half lengthways and use a spoon to scoop out the seeds.

3 Spoon some of the rice into the hollowed-out cucumber halves and press down gently to pack the rice into the cucumber.

4 Fill with the tuna mixture, then sprinkle with a little more of the seasoning.

5 Cut each cucumber half into 6 or 7 smaller sushi boats.

IN CASE OF EMERGENCY

As a parent, you know that sometimes meal times sneak up on you, and you're left scrambling to find something quick. Whether you're late home from work, you have a last-minute school event, or the kids just won't stop asking for snacks, I've got you covered with simple, creative recipes that can be whipped up in no time. These meals are designed to save you when you need to feed the family fast. They are designed for emergency situations, offering minimal prep time, accessible ingredients and a few clever shortcuts. So take a deep breath and let's handle those hectic moments with stress-free, delicious snacks and meals!

PIZZA ROLL UPS

If you're looking for a pizza fix and want something quick and easy to make for the kids then this is a must try – it's proper tasty!

MAKES 4

-

4 tablespoons Red Sauce (see page 166) or ready-made pizza sauce, plus extra if needed

4 mini soft flour tortillas

100–150g (3½–5½oz) Cheddar cheese, grated

12 slices of pepperoni

4 cheese strings or strips of mozzarella

4 tablespoons garlic and herb butter, melted

1 Preheat the air fryer to 180°C, or the oven to 180°C (400°F), Gas Mark 6. Spread a spoonful of the sauce over each tortilla, leaving a small border around the edges.

2 Scatter grated Cheddar over the sauce and arrange 3 pepperoni slices across the middle of each.

3 Place a cheese string on top of the pepperoni for that stretchy goodness. If using mozzarella, cut strips to size.

4 Tightly roll the tortillas, adding a little extra tomato sauce if you need it to help hold the tortillas together.

5 Brush the tortillas with the garlic and herb butter for more flavour. Cook in the air fryer or oven for 6–8 minutes, until golden.

TOASTER POCKET WRAP

Over 45 million people liked my toaster pocket wrap and once you try it you'll see why! It's a brilliant hack that I didn't know I needed in order to be a mum. You fill a tortilla with your fillings, fold it three times and pop it in the toaster – it's as simple as that.

Get inventive with your fillings. Why not try tuna, thinly sliced mushrooms or tomatoes, or hummus? Just remember not to overload it or the cheese won't melt.

SERVES 1

–

1 soft flour tortilla
2 slices of ham
1 large slice of cheese,
    torn in half
butter (optional)

1 Lay the tortilla on a board and arrange the slices of ham on top.

2 Top the ham with the cheese.

3 Wrap one side of the tortilla over the fillings.

4 Wrap the other side over the fillings to enclose completely.

5 Fold the wrap in half to create 2 pockets. Toast in the toaster, open sides up, until golden, or fry in a knob of butter in a frying pan until crisp.

EGG IN A HOLE WITH A SWEET TREAT

When I was growing up, eggs and toast was our go-to quick meal when we were hungry. But here's a way to get a sweet treat out of it, too!

If you prefer, fill the bread discs with a small spoon of jam or peanut butter before folding and sealing!

SERVES 2
-
2 slices of bread
butter
2 eggs
2 squares of chocolate
   – I used Kinder
salt and pepper

1 If using, preheat the air fryer to 200°C. Use a round cookie cutter to cut a hole out of the middle of each slice of bread.

2 Heat a little butter in a large frying pan with a lid over a low-medium heat and fry the bread until golden underneath.

3 Flip the bread over and crack an egg in the middle of each slice. Put a lid on the pan and cook the egg to your liking, then season with salt and pepper.

4 While that's cooking, place the squares of chocolate on the discs of bread. Fold the bread over and use the tines of a fork to seal the edges.

5 Spread a little butter on each side of the sweet treats and fry in the pan with the eggs or cook in the air fryer for 4–6 minutes until golden.

SWEET CHILLI HALLOUMI CRISPS

This one is so handy! All you need is a good vegetable peeler, a block of halloumi and some sweet chilli sauce. Great when the kids want a snack or something crispy on the side.

There are plenty of different flavouring options you could try. Honey works well, or mix up some paprika, dried herbs and salt and pepper with a little oil and brush that on instead.

SERVES 4
-
225g (8oz) halloumi
  cheese
2 tablespoons sweet
  chilli sauce
salt and pepper

1 Preheat the oven to 200°C (425°F), Gas Mark 7. Use a vegetable peeler to slice the halloumi into thin pieces, about 5mm (¼ inch) thick.

2 Line a baking tray with baking paper and arrange the halloumi slices on it in a single layer.

3 Brush with the sweet chilli sauce and sprinkle over some seasoning if you wish.

4 Cook in the oven for 15–20 minutes, until the halloumi is golden and crispy on the edges.

SALAMI ROSE WRAPS

Lunches can get boring so why not create this quick and easy wrap for the kids? Great in an emergency when you've forgotten to get something nice for a school trip or if your child's having a hard time at school and you want to cheer up their lunchbox.

MAKES 4
-
1 soft flour tortilla
cheese spread or butter
12 slices of salami,
   halved
4 basil leaves

1 Cut the tortilla into 4–6 strips, depending on the size of your salami slices. Spread 4 of the strips with cream cheese or butter.

2 Arrange 6 pieces of salami on each strip in a line, slightly overlapping each other.

3 Roll the tortilla strips and, when you get to the end, add a basil leaf for that extra touch.

PANCAKE MUFFINS

Did you know you can make muffins with pancake batter? And even better, they freeze well – just heat them up or defrost for an emergency after-school snack or lunch. You could even buy ready-made pancake batter mix for an even faster result.

MAKES 12

-

1 quantity of Fluffy Pancake Mix (see page 171)
butter, for greasing

TOPPING IDEAS
blueberries
raspberries
chocolate chips
grated cheese
sun-dried tomatoes
grated courgette
grated carrot
salt and pepper

1 Preheat the oven to 200°C (425°F), Gas Mark 7, and grease a 12-hole muffin tin with butter. Pour the batter into the muffin holes until about three-quarters full.

2 Add your toppings and cook in the oven for 12–15 minutes, until risen and golden.

TOASTIE ROLL-UPS

Toastie roll-ups are – no surprises – rolled-up sandwiches, dipped in egg and fried. You can customize them with any sweet or savoury fillings you like. The kids can help choose fillings, roll the sandwiches and dip them in the egg. The filling possibilities are endless!

MAKES 2

-

2 slices of bread
butter
1 slice of ham
handful of grated
  Cheddar cheese
1 tablespoon cream
  cheese
1 tablespoon jam mixed
  with a few crushed
  blueberries
1 egg, beaten

Serve them whole for bigger kids or slice them into pinwheels for little ones who prefer finger foods.

1 Place the slices of bread on a board and use a rolling pin to flatten them out.

2 Butter one of the slices and top with the ham and cheese. Spread the other slice with the cream cheese and top with the jam and blueberries.

3 Roll up the sandwiches tightly and seal by pressing the tines of a fork against the open ends.

You can season the beaten egg with salt, dried herbs and spices, or sugar and cinnamon if you like.

4 Place the beaten egg in a shallow bowl and turn the rolls in it to coat them all over.

5 Heat a knob of butter in a frying pan over a medium heat and fry the rolls on all sides, for about 1–2 minutes, until golden all over.

CHICKEN TORTILLA SAMOSAS

A good samosa takes a lot of time to make, especially if you're creating it from scratch. Here we turn leftover chicken and a few veg into a quick tasty meal the kids will be excited for. We have been doing this for the longest time and it is honestly a lifesaver.

MAKES 4

-

150g (5½oz) cooked meat, chopped

½ red pepper, cored, deseeded and diced

150g (5½oz) sweetcorn

½ onion, finely diced

50g (1¾oz) spinach, chopped

100g (3½oz) Cheddar cheese, grated

3 tablespoons mayonnaise

1 teaspoon plain flour

2 soft flour tortillas, halved

vegetable oil

I used leftover spicy chicken, but any cooked meat will do, even minced meat. If you don't have leftovers, use ready-cooked meat from the supermarket.

Tuna mayonnaise is another good filling option, or try a veggie version using leftover cooked potatoes.

1 Preheat the air fryer to 180°C, or the oven to 180°C (400°F), Gas Mark 6. Mix the meat with the veg, cheese and mayo.

2 Place some filling on one side of each tortilla half, taking care not to overfill!

3 Make your glue by mixing the flour with a little water to form a paste. Drizzle a little of the glue round the edges of the tortillas.

4 Fold over the tortillas and press firmly round the edges of the samosas with your fingers or the tines of a fork to seal them, then spray with a little bit of oil.

5 Cook in the air fryer or oven for 5–10 minutes, until the outsides are crispy and the filling is heated through. You could also gently shallow fry them until golden on both sides.

GOOEY CORNFLAKE BITES

These gooey, stretchy, cheesy bites are perfect when the kids are in need of a fun snack.

You can season the flour with pepper, garlic granules, paprika or dried herbs if you like, too.

MAKES 3

-

2 tablespoons plain flour
pinch of salt
1 egg, beaten
100g (3½oz) plain or
   honey nut cornflakes,
   crushed
3 Mini Babybel cheeses
vegetable oil

1 Preheat the air fryer to 180°C, or the oven to 180°C (400°F), Gas Mark 6. Mix the flour and salt in one bowl, place the egg in another and the cornflakes in a third. Dip the cheeses in the flour to coat.

2 Now turn the cheeses in the egg until coated all over.

3 Finally, dip them in the crushed cornflakes until fully coated, then spray with a light coating of oil.

4 Cook for 5–8 minutes in the air fryer or 5–10 minutes in the oven, until crispy. You could also gently shallow fry them until golden on both sides.

CRISPY PARMESAN BROCCOLI

I created this banging recipe when my son decided he wasn't keen on broccoli any more. This changed his mind and he found his love for broccoli again. With over 63 million views on Instagram and 18.6 million on TikTok, it seems lots of other people have also rekindled their love for this humble veg!

SERVES 2–3
-
1 head of broccoli, cut
   into florets
2 tablespoons olive oil
6 tablespoons grated
   Parmesan cheese,
   plus a little extra for
   sprinkling

SEASONING OPTIONS
ground cumin
dried oregano
garlic granules
paprika
all-purpose seasoning
salt and pepper

1 Preheat the air fryer to 185°C, or the oven to 185°C (400°F), Gas Mark 6. Boil the broccoli florets in a pan of salted water for 5–15 minutes until softened, depending on size. Drain well.

2 Mix your seasonings of choice with the olive oil and drizzle on a baking tray lined with baking paper. Count your broccoli florets and make the same number of mounds of cheese on the tray.

3 Place the broccoli florets on the cheese and gently smash them flat using the base of a glass.

Let the florets rest for a few minutes after cooking and they will become nice and crispy.

4 Sprinkle each floret with a little more Parmesan and some seasoning.

5 Cook in the air fryer or oven for 15–30 minutes, until the edges are crispy. Cooking time will depend on the size of the florets.

DINNER TIME

When it comes to dinner, we all want something that's not only satisfying but also a little different. Our children can get bored with the same meals over and over again, so this chapter is filled with creative recipe ideas, each designed to add some fun and flair to your usual repertoire. From simple comfort foods with surprising twists to globally inspired dishes that bring new flavours to your table, I hope every recipe sparks excitement and brings you a fresh take on familiar favourites. Prepare to be inspired and add a dash of creativity to your mealtime routine!

ROAST DINNER KEBAB

Change up your roast dinners with this delicious, easy twist on a British classic. The shawarma-style chicken comes out super-tender with crispy edges every time. Perfect for guests or when you want something a little different.

SERVES 4
-
1kg (2lb 4oz) boneless chicken thighs
4 tablespoons melted butter
3 garlic cloves, thinly sliced
2 tablespoons vegetable oil
125ml (4fl oz) water
4 carrots, cut into chunks
2 large potatoes, cut into chunks
300g (10½oz) sprouts, trimmed
gravy and Yorkshire puddings, to serve

SPICE MIX
2 teaspoons dried oregano
2 teaspoons paprika
2 teaspoons garlic granules
2 teaspoons all-purpose seasoning
2 teaspoons dried thyme or rosemary
salt and pepper

1 Mix all the ingredients for the spice mix in a small bowl. Place the chicken thighs in a mixing bowl with the melted butter, garlic and 2 tablespoons of the spice mix, turn well to coat and marinate in the refrigerator for a few hours or overnight.

2 Remove the chicken from the refrigerator 30 minutes before cooking. Preheat the oven to 180°C (400°F), Gas Mark 6.

3 Mix the vegetable oil with the chicken and layer it onto a kebab spike. If you don't have a kebab spike, insert a skewer into a large potato or half an onion. Stand the spike in a large oven dish and add the measured water. Season the prepared veggies with the remaining spice mix and place in the dish under the chicken.

4 Cook in the oven for 1–1½ hours, or until the chicken and veg are cooked through, stirring the vegetables occasionally and adding more oil or water if needed. Serve with gravy and Yorkshire puddings.

For a vegetarian version, swap the chicken for portobello mushrooms and red onion.

VIBRANT VEGGIE RICE

Enjoy this flavourful vegetable rice as a side dish or a meal in itself. Feel free to adjust the seasoning and spice levels based on your family's preferences. Whatever size your mug or cup, the key ratio to remember is one of rice and one of veg to two of water.

SERVES 4

-

2 tablespoons oil
   or butter, plus
   1 tablespoon butter
   to serve (optional)
2 fresh curry leaves
½ onion, diced
1 teaspoon mild Madras
   curry powder
1 teaspoon ground turmeric
1 teaspoon all-purpose
   seasoning
1 large mug of basmati rice
2 large mugs of water
1 large mug of frozen mixed
   vegetables
salt and pepper

1 Heat the oil or butter in a pan with a lid over a medium heat and add the curry leaves, onion and spices. Cook gently until the onion softens slightly, about 10 minutes.

2 Rinse the rice in cold water until the water runs clear to remove excess starch. Add the rice, measured water and frozen veg to the pan and season to taste. Bring it to the boil, lower the heat to a simmer and cover with a lid.

3 Let it simmer for 15–20 minutes, until the rice is cooked (adding more water if necessary) and the water has been absorbed. Once the rice is cooked, fluff it up with a fork and stir through the extra butter, if liked, before serving.

BEEF & BROCCOLI NOODLES

These Mongolian-style noodles make a quick and tasty meal in 30 minutes – they're absolutely banging every time. Try it with rice instead of noodles for an alternative option. Either way, this brilliant dish will have everyone asking for seconds.

You can adjust the amount of water, depending on how thick or thin you like your sauce.

SERVES 4

-

350g (12oz) flank or skirt steak, thinly sliced

70g (2½oz) cornflour, plus extra for coating

2 tablespoons vegetable oil

2 tablespoons sesame oil

1 onion, roughly chopped

1 tablespoon crushed garlic

1 teaspoon garlic granules

½ teaspoon grated fresh root ginger

2 tablespoons oyster sauce

125ml (4fl oz) dark soy sauce

125ml (4fl oz) water

90g (3¼oz) dark soft brown sugar

generous splash of liquid seasoning

pinch of chilli flakes (optional)

200g (7oz) cooked tenderstem broccoli

600g (1lb 5oz) cooked egg noodles

2–3 spring onions, finely chopped

1 tablespoon sesame seeds

salt and pepper

1 Place the steak in a bowl, dust with cornflour and toss to coat it all over. Heat half the vegetable oil and sesame oil in a wok or frying pan over a medium-high heat until very hot, then add the steak and stir-fry for 3–5 minutes, until just cooked to your liking. Remove from the pan and set aside.

2 Reheat the pan and add the remaining oil. Add the onion, garlic, garlic granules, ginger, oyster sauce, soy sauce, measured water, sugar, liquid seasoning, salt, pepper and chilli flakes, if using. Cook over a medium heat for 10–20 minutes, or until the sauce starts to thicken.

3 Add the cooked steak and broccoli, stir well and cook for 1–2 minutes to reheat them.

4 Stir in the noodles, ensuring they are coated in the sauce, and cook for a couple of minutes more. Sprinkle with the spring onion and sesame seeds and enjoy!

HASSELBACK SALMON & VEG TRAYBAKE

Cooking salmon in the oven on a bed of delicious veggies soaks up the flavours and results in perfectly cooked salmon every time.

You can mix up the vegetables here, using whatever your family prefers. Try chopped courgettes and cherry tomatoes for a nice summery combo.

SERVES 4

-

4 boneless salmon fillets

150g (5½oz) fine green
beans, trimmed

1 head of broccoli, cut
into florets

1 red pepper, cored,
deseeded and cut into
chunks

1 small onion, diced

2 small lemons, sliced

6 thyme sprigs

2 tablespoons olive oil

salt and pepper

FOR THE POTATOES

8–10 small potatoes, cut
into chunks

1 teaspoon dried oregano

2 teaspoons garlic
granules

3–4 tablespoons
vegetable or olive oil

SEASONING

1 tablespoon all-purpose
seasoning

1 teaspoon ground cumin

1 teaspoon paprika

a few splashes of liquid
seasoning

1 tablespoon crushed
garlic

2–3 teaspoons barbecue
seasoning

1 tablespoon soy sauce

1 tablespoon water

1 Preheat the oven to 200°C
(425°F), Gas Mark 7. Place all the
potato ingredients in a large
roasting tin and season well. Cook
in the oven for 15–20 minutes.

2 Make a series of cuts into each
salmon fillet, spacing them
0.5–1cm (¼–½ inch) apart. Be
careful not to cut through the skin!

3 Mix all the seasoning
ingredients together in a small
bowl to make a lovely marinade.
Use a brush to coat the salmon
fillets all over, saving a little
marinade for the veg.

4 Tip the vegetables into the
potato dish, add the remaining
marinade and mix well. Arrange
the salmon, lemon and thyme on
top and drizzle with oil. Cook for
20–30 minutes in the oven, until
the veg is tender, then serve.

TACO CUPS

Here's another great way to use tortillas. These Mexican-style taco cups are fun to make and my boys love them as they are small and easy to eat. Serve with some simple chopped vegetables for dinner, or as a tasty appetizer or packed lunch. You can also pop them in the freezer to bring out when you don't fancy cooking!

1 Place the onion, minced beef, garlic and spices in a pan over a medium heat and cook, stirring regularly, until the meat is browned and the onion is softened. Add the tomato purée, bay leaves and black beans, and cook for a further 15 minutes, adding a little water if it starts to catch. Add the red pepper and cook for another 10–15 minutes, until softened, then season with salt and pepper.

Try different fillings in these cups, such as leftover Bolognese. Or what about making roti cups using Homemade Roti (see page 170) filled with my Don't Worry Chicken Curry (see page 100)?

2 Preheat the oven to 200°C (425°F), Gas Mark 7. Cut discs out of the tortillas using a cookie cutter or by cutting round a small bowl with a knife. Press the discs into the holes in a 12-hole muffin tray (no need to grease it first).

3 Alternatively, you can cut the tortillas into quarters and use the quarters to make the muffin cups. Just press them into the holes in the same way.

4 Fill the cups with the filling of your choice (1–2 tablespoons of filling per cup) and press it down well.

5 Top the cups with a good layer of grated cheese, then cook in the oven for 15–20 minutes, or until golden.

MAKES 12

-

3 soft flour tortillas
filling of your choice (try my Beef Filling below)
175g (6oz) Cheddar and Red Leicester cheese, grated
chopped cucumber, tomatoes and peppers, to serve

BEEF FILLING

1 onion, diced
500g (1lb 2oz) minced beef
2 tablespoons crushed garlic
1 tablespoon paprika
1 tablespoon dried oregano
2 tablespoons ground cumin
2 tablespoons tomato purée
2 bay leaves
200g (7oz) can black beans, rinsed and drained
1 red pepper, cored, deseeded and chopped
salt and pepper

Use any leftover scraps of tortilla to make tortilla chips (see page 157).

GIANT PIG IN A BLANKET

Imagine taking this out of your oven for a family dinner! Served with my fluffy mash and peas, it's a proper hearty meal at any time, but would also make an amazing Christmas showstopper.

SERVES 4

-

8 linked Cumberland
    sausages
12 streaky bacon rashers
peas, to serve

FLUFFY MASH
1kg (2lb 4oz) baking
    potatoes, peeled and
    quartered
2 tablespoons cream
    cheese
50g (1¾oz) butter
1 tablespoon garlic
    granules
1–2 teaspoons dried
    thyme
150–200ml (5–7fl oz)
    milk
salt and garlic pepper

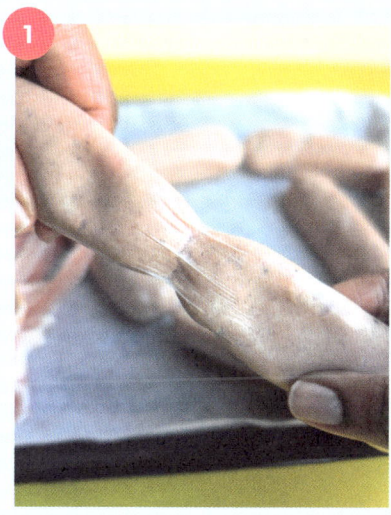

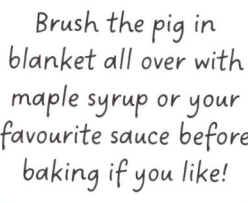

Brush the pig in blanket all over with maple syrup or your favourite sauce before baking if you like!

1 Preheat the oven to 200°C (425°F), Gas Mark 7. Line a baking tray with baking paper. Untwist the sausage casing, pushing meat into the gaps.

2 Wrap the rashers of bacon in a spiral fashion around the sausage, covering it as well as possible.

3 Roll up the bacon-wrapped sausage into a tight coil on the baking tray.

4 Cook in the preheated oven for 30–40 minutes, until golden and cooked through. It will get messy while cooking, so carefully pour the excess oil away halfway through cooking time.

5 Meanwhile, boil the potatoes in salted water until soft, then drain and mash. Add the cream cheese, butter, garlic granules and thyme, season to taste, then beat in the milk a little at a time, until the mash is smooth and fluffy. Serve with the pig in blanket and peas.

HALLOUMI & MEDITERRANEAN VEG BAKE

I love grilled halloumi and at home we like to mix it up with some colourful summer vegetables. This vibrant traybake takes around 30 minutes to make and it's healthy and delicious.

SERVES 4

-
1 courgette, cut into
   chunks
1 yellow pepper, cored,
   deseeded and cut into
   chunks
1 red onion, cut into
   chunks
1 teaspoon dried
   oregano
1 teaspoon dried thyme
1 teaspoon dried basil
1 teaspoon paprika
1 teaspoon ground cumin
1 teaspoon garlic granules
1 teaspoon harissa paste
   (optional)
1 teaspoon garlic paste
2 tablespoons olive oil
450g (1lb) halloumi
   cheese, sliced
225g (8oz) cherry
   tomatoes on the vine
salt and pepper

Flip over the slices of halloumi halfway through cooking if you want both sides really golden.

TOMATO STOCK
1 vegetable stock cube
150ml (¼ pint) boiling
   water
2 tablespoons honey
2 tablespoons tomato
   purée

Serve this traybake as a side dish, or keep it simple and just serve with some crusty bread.

1 Preheat the oven to 200°C (425°F), Gas Mark 7. Place all the vegetables into an oven dish or roasting tin and add all the herbs and spices.

2 Next add the harissa paste, if using, the garlic paste and the olive oil. Season with salt and pepper.

3 Mix all the tomato stock ingredients together in a small bowl and pour over the vegetables.

4 Mix everything together, then spread out in the dish or tin in an even layer.

5 Top with the slices of halloumi and the cherry tomatoes, season to taste and cook in the oven for 20–30 minutes, until the halloumi is golden.

SMASHED LAMB TACOS

I used minced lamb to make these tasty flatbreads, but minced chicken or beef work just as well. With potato wedges and a simple salad, this flavourful recipe makes a really tasty dinner everyone will enjoy.

MAKES 6

-

400g (14oz) minced lamb
1 tablespoon ground cumin
1 tablespoon paprika
1 tablespoon dried oregano
1 tablespoon chopped fresh coriander
1 tablespoon dried thyme
1 tablespoon garam masala
1 tablespoon harissa paste
1 tablespoon garlic paste
1 tablespoon ginger paste
6 mini soft flour tortillas
salt and pepper

TO SERVE
potato wedges
shredded lettuce
sliced cucumber
sliced tomatoes
mayonnaise

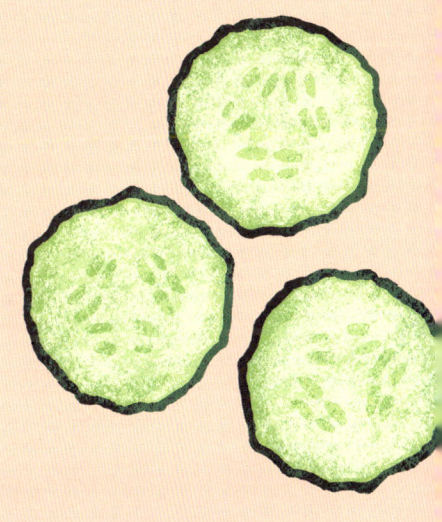

1 Place the meat in a bowl, add all the spices, herbs and pastes, season to taste, then mix with your hands until everything is well combined. Place a handful of the meat on each tortilla.

2 Flatten the seasoned meat into a nice thin and even layer. Spread it out right to the edges of the tortillas as it will shrink during cooking.

I have used mini tortillas here, but any kind of flatbread works. Simply spread the meat on one side and fry until the meat is golden and cooked through.

3 Heat a frying pan over a low-medium heat and add one of the tortillas, meat side down. Fry gently for 4–7 minutes, pressing down with a spatula, until the meat is golden.

4 Flip it over and fry for 3–5 more minutes, until the bread is crispy and the meat cooked through (cut into it to check it is cooked – the cooking time will depend on how thick the meat is). Repeat with the other tortillas. Serve with potato wedges, salad and mayonnaise.

SMASHED POTATO & VEGETABLE TART

This is not just a recipe, it's an experience that will bring comfort and creativity to your table! Whether you're serving it as a main or a stunning side, this savoury tart will have everyone asking for more.

SERVES 4–6

-

3 whole baking
    potatoes, skin on and
    cut into quarters
4 tablespoons garlic
    butter, melted
½ courgette, grated
½ large carrot, grated
½ red pepper, cored,
    deseeded and finely
    chopped
½ onion, thinly sliced
100g (3½oz) sweetcorn
140g (5oz) mature
    Cheddar cheese,
    grated
fresh coriander, to
    garnish

Let the tart cool for 5–10 minutes after cooking to make it easier to slice and serve.

CREAM MIXTURE

300ml (½ pint) double
  cream
1 tablespoon garlic
  granules
1 tablespoon plain flour
1 teaspoon dried
  oregano
1 tablespoon paprika
1 teaspoon ground
  coriander
1 teaspoon ground cumin
salt and pepper

1 Preheat the oven to 200°C (425°F), Gas Mark 7. Boil the potatoes in salted water until soft, about 15 minutes, then drain. Place them in a nonstick tart tin and flatten them with the bottom of a glass to form an even layer.

2 Drizzle the melted garlic butter over the smashed potatoes, then use a fork to mix and press the mixture down firmly, making sure the bottom and sides of the tin are evenly covered.

3 Add the courgette, carrot, red pepper, onion, sweetcorn and half the grated cheese. Stir everything together, spread it out evenly and flatten it into the tin.

4 In a separate bowl, whisk together all the ingredients for the cream mixture until smooth and well combined. Slowly pour the cream mixture over the vegetables, ensuring it covers the filling evenly.

5 Sprinkle over the remaining grated cheese and bake in the oven for 45 minutes–1 hour, or until the top is golden and the filling is set. Garnish with fresh coriander before serving.

CHICKEN FAJITA SLIDERS

Fajitas are always a winner at dinner, and so are burgers – so why not combine the two with my fajita sliders? They're a win-win!

MAKES 6

-

1 tablespoon vegetable oil

1 onion, chopped

2 garlic cloves, chopped

600g (1lb 5oz) chicken breast fillets, cut into small chunks

1 tablespoon paprika

1 tablespoon ground cumin

1 tablespoon all-purpose seasoning

1 tablespoon dried oregano

1 teaspoon ground coriander

½ red pepper, cored, deseeded and chopped

½ orange pepper, cored, deseeded and chopped

juice of 1 lime

handful of fresh coriander, chopped

6 burger buns

ready-made sour cream and chive sauce

200g (7oz) mozzarella cheese, grated

salt and pepper

GLAZE
2 tablespoons butter, melted
pinch of garlic granules
1 tablespoon chopped fresh coriander

Serve with extra sour cream and chive sauce on the side for dipping.

1 Heat the oil in a pan over medium heat. Add the onion and garlic and sauté until softened. Add the chicken to the pan with the spices and dried herbs, and season with salt and pepper. Cook for about 10 minutes, until browned.

2 Add the chopped peppers and squeeze in the lime juice. Cook for another 10 minutes, until the peppers are tender. Stir in the fresh coriander and remove from the heat. Preheat the oven to 180°C (400°F), Gas Mark 6.

3 Slice the buns in half and place the bottom halves on a baking tray. Spread sour cream and chive sauce on the buns, then sprinkle half the mozzarella on top.

4 Spoon the chicken mixture over the buns, add another drizzle of sour cream and chive sauce, then top with the remaining mozzarella and the bun lids.

5 Mix the glaze ingredients together in a bowl, then brush it over the tops of the buns. Bake in the oven for 15–20 minutes, or until the buns are slightly crispy and the cheese has melted.

DON'T WORRY CHICKEN CURRY

This one is for when you want something tasty, but don't have time to keep an eye on the cooker. Just bang this one-pot curry in the oven – it comes out perfect every time.

SERVES 4

-

650g (1lb 7oz) boneless, skinless chicken thighs, cut into chunks

1 large baking potato, cut into 2cm (¾ inch) pieces

1 teaspoon ground cumin

2 tablespoons mild Madras curry powder

1 tablespoon garam masala

½ teaspoon ground turmeric

1 teaspoon paprika

6–8 dried curry leaves

1 tablespoon tomato purée

2 tablespoons crushed garlic

250ml (9fl oz) natural yogurt

1 teaspoon garlic granules

juice of ½ lemon

½ onion, chopped

salt and pepper

fresh coriander, to garnish

rice or Homemade Roti (see page 170), to serve

You can prepare
this the night before to
save even more time. Just mix
it all together in the oven dish,
cover with foil and place in the
refrigerator until you are ready
to cook. The next day, simply
pop it in the oven to
finish.

1 Preheat the oven to 200°C (425°F), Gas Mark 7. Put the chicken and potatoes in an oven dish or roasting tin.

2 Add the spices, curry leaves, tomato purée and crushed garlic.

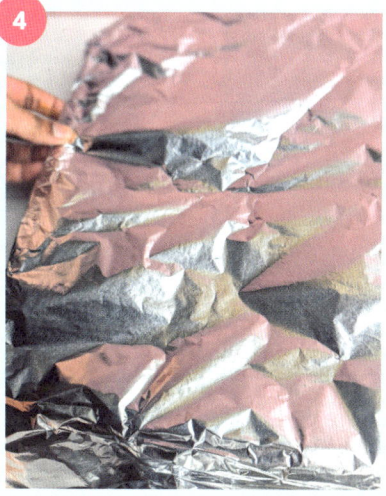

3 Pour in the yogurt, add the garlic granules and some salt and pepper and squeeze the lemon juice on top. Add the onion and mix well.

4 Cover the dish with kitchen foil. Use a large piece that will cover the dish securely and trap all the steam during cooking.

5 Cook in the oven for about 1 hour, until the vegetables are tender and the chicken is cooked through. Garnish with fresh coriander and serve with rice or roti.

CHICKEN, CAULIFLOWER & BROCCOLI PIE

This recipe is fun and interactive, allowing the kids to use cookie or Play-Doh cutters to cut shapes out of the puff pastry while you prepare the filling. The pie itself is hearty, comforting and dreamy.

SERVES 4–6
-
2 tablespoons vegetable oil

½ white onion, sliced

600g (1lb 5oz) boneless chicken breast, sliced

1 tablespoon garlic granules

1 tablespoon paprika

1 tablespoon dried oregano

1 tablespoon all-purpose seasoning

200g (7oz) broccoli florets

200g (7oz) cauliflower florets

300ml (½ pint) double cream

100g (3½oz) Cheddar cheese, grated

325g (11½oz) ready-rolled puff pastry

1 egg, beaten

salt and pepper

1 Heat the vegetable oil in a large pan over a medium heat. Add the onion and chicken, and fry for a few minutes until the chicken starts to cook. Sprinkle in the garlic granules, paprika, oregano and all-purpose seasoning, stir well and cook for 14 minutes, stirring occasionally.

2 Add the broccoli and cauliflower, followed by the double cream. Stir, cover the pan and cook for 10–15 minutes, stirring occasionally, until the vegetables have softened a little. Season to taste, add the cheese and stir until melted.

3 Preheat the oven to 200°C (425°F), Gas Mark 7. Unroll the puff pastry and get the kids to cut out all types of shapes using cutters.

4 Transfer the creamy chicken to an oven dish or roasting tin. Arrange the puff pastry shapes on top, overlapping each other.

5 Brush the pastry with beaten egg and cook in the oven for 20–30 minutes, until the puff pastry is golden on top.

ROLL-UP VEGGIE LASAGNE

One of my classic hacks and a firm favourite at home, this fun twist on lasagne may not be traditional, but it's so good. It's also a great way to make individual portions if you're making lasagne for a big group of family and friends.

SERVES 6
-
2 tablespoons vegetable oil
1 onion, diced
2–4 garlic cloves, chopped
1 teaspoon paprika
1 teaspoon ground cumin
1 teaspoon all-purpose seasoning
2 teaspoons dried mixed herbs
400g (14oz) can chopped tomatoes
1 vegetable stock cube
500g (1lb 2oz) frozen mixed vegetables
300g (10½oz) fresh lasagne sheets, halved lengthways
450g (1lb) ready-made white sauce
400g (14oz) mixed grated mozzarella and Cheddar
50g (1¾oz) Parmesan cheese, grated
salt and pepper

1 Put the oil, onion, garlic, spices, herbs and tomatoes into a large pan and crumble in the stock cube. Bring to the boil over a medium heat and simmer for 10–15 minutes until thickened slightly.

2 Toss in the frozen vegetables and mix well. Cook for 10 minutes more until the vegetables are tender and the sauce is well combined. Preheat the oven to 200°C (425°F), Gas Mark 7.

3 Lay the lasagne sheets on a board, spread a spoonful of white sauce onto each sheet, then sprinkle on some grated mozzarella and Cheddar.

4 Spoon some of the vegetable mix over the cheese on each sheet then, starting from one end, carefully roll each lasagne sheet up tightly, securing the filling inside.

5 Place another spoonful of the white sauce and the vegetable mixture in a large oven dish and spread out to coat the base. Place the lasagne rolls side by side in the dish.

6 Spread the remaining white sauce and vegetable mixture over the rolls and sprinkle the remaining grated mozzarella and Cheddar on top along with the Parmesan. Cook in the oven for 45 minutes–1 hour, until golden and bubbling.

SWEET TREATS

Everyone loves a little something sweet now and then, right? The next few pages are all about fun, quirky treats perfect for anyone with a sweet tooth. These recipes bring a little extra joy to your day – many of them are affordable and you probably have most of the ingredients in your kitchen right now. From familiar favourites with a twist to some totally unique ideas, these sweet fixes are sure to hit the spot. So, grab what you've got in the kitchen or pop to the shops and let's make some treats that will bring smiles all round!

THREE-INGREDIENT LAVA CAKES

That's right, all you need is three ingredients. We always have chocolate in our house and I turn to this recipe when we have guests over and I forgot pudding, or when we have lots of chocolate left over from special occasions like Easter and Christmas.

MAKES 2
-
85g (3oz) milk chocolate, plus extra for the centres
30g (1oz) plain flour
1 egg

Don't worry if your chocolate centres aren't gooey, as I have a trick. The tops of the cakes are usually cracked, so slip some extra pieces of chocolate inside to melt, or just lay some on top for a gooey topping.

1 Preheat the air fryer to 160°C, or the oven to 160°C (350°F), Gas Mark 4. Place the chocolate in a microwavable bowl and melt it in the microwave on full power for 60–90 seconds, checking halfway through and stirring well.

2 Add the flour and egg and mix with a fork or whisk until everything is nice and smooth.

3 Divide the mixture between 2 small heatproof ramekins or glass dessert pots.

4 Push 2 or 3 extra squares of chocolate into the centre of each pudding, making sure they are covered by the cake batter.

5 Bake in the air fryer or oven for 13 minutes, until the cake mixture is risen and golden on top.

BANANA & STRAWBERRY CROFFLES

Watching a movie and fancy a sweet snack? Or have you just got a sweet tooth and a mid-afternoon craving for a treat? Either way, I've got you.

Serve the croffles with whipped cream or ice cream for extra decadence!

MAKES 2

-

2 croissants
8 squares of chocolate or
   2 small chocolate bars
1 banana, sliced
handful of strawberries,
   chopped
icing sugar, for
   sprinkling

1 Split the croissants in half but don't cut all the way through.

2 Place 4 squares of chocolate or 1 small chocolate bar in each croissant.

3 Arrange the sliced banana on top of the chocolate in one croissant and the chopped strawberries in the other.

4 Place them in a waffle maker and cook for 2–4 minutes or until golden.

5 Check the chocolate has melted, giving them a little extra time if not. To serve, sprinkle with icing sugar and top with any leftover fruit.

CHOCOLATE FLOWER POPS

Need an activity to keep the kids busy for a little while? Here's an easy and cute idea with a little sweet treat at the end.

MAKES 2

-

6 squares of milk chocolate
8 Smarties
1 strawberry, sliced

1 Place the chocolate in a microwavable bowl and melt it in the microwave on full power for 30–60 seconds, checking halfway through and stirring well.

2 Line a chopping board or plate with baking paper and arrange 2 lolly sticks on it. Spoon the melted chocolate over the tops of the sticks to make 2 round puddles.

3 Arrange the Smarties and strawberry slices on the chocolate to make flowers. Place in the refrigerator for 2–3 hours to harden.

STRAWBERRY CLUSTERS

A fun and refreshing snack, perfect for spring and summer days. This is ideal as an after-school treat or a delicious dessert.

MAKES 3

-

5 large strawberries, sliced

3 tablespoons yogurt

100g (3½oz) milk chocolate, melted and stirred well

Choose your favourite yogurt – honey and vanilla both go well here.

Any type of chocolate will work, and feel free to customize your clusters with a sprinkling of nuts or granola.

1 Arrange the strawberry slices on a sheet of baking paper to make 3 flower shapes. Finely chop any remaining strawberry pieces and use to fill in the centres.

2 Place a spoonful of yogurt on top of each cluster, covering the strawberries and forming a creamy base.

3 Spoon the melted chocolate over the yogurt and transfer the clusters to the freezer for at least 2 hours, or until firm.

CHURRO-STYLE CRUMPETS

I love churros – there's something about them, right? Every mouthful is just so moreish and delicious. Here I upgrade some affordable crumpets into a churro-style sweet treat using ingredients you've probably got in your cupboard – all in under 15 minutes.

Serve hot with a dip of your choice – we like melted milk chocolate mixed with Biscoff spread.

SERVES 2
-
2 crumpets, cut into fingers
2 tablespoons melted butter
3–4 teaspoons caster sugar
1 teaspoon ground cinnamon

1 Preheat the air fryer to 180°C, or the oven to 200°C (425°F), Gas Mark 7. Toss the crumpet sticks with the melted butter until coated all over.

2 Mix the sugar and cinnamon in a small bowl and sprinkle three-quarters of the mixture over the crumpet sticks and toss again.

3 Cook in the air fryer or oven for 5–10 minutes, until crispy. Sprinkle with the remaining cinnamon sugar for that final touch.

CUSTARD TART CRUMPETS

Think crumpets, custard tart style! Sweeten up your crumpets with these simple steps to make a quick, affordable and delicious dessert.

MAKES 2

-

2 crumpets

2–3 tablespoons ready-made custard

1 dessertspoon sugar

1 Preheat the air fryer to 180°C, or the oven to 200°C (425°F), Gas Mark 7. Place each crumpet on a small square of baking paper.

2 Use a small sharp knife to cut a circle into the top of each crumpet, being careful not to cut all the way through. Hollow out the middles of the crumpets to make tart cases.

3 Spoon the custard into the hollows in the crumpets, filling them up to the top.

4 Sprinkle the sugar over the top of the custard and cook in the air fryer or oven for 10–13 minutes, or until golden.

NO-CHURN STRAWBERRY ICE CREAM

This easy ice cream is made without any special equipment, just a few simple ingredients and lots of anticipation!

SERVES 6–8

-

200g (7oz) strawberries, hulled

1 tablespoon caster sugar (optional)

240ml (8½fl oz) double cream

397g (14oz) can sweetened condensed milk

juice of ½–1 lemon

1–2 teaspoons vanilla extract

1 Place the strawberries in a blender or food processor with the sugar, if using, and whizz until smooth. If you prefer some texture in your ice cream, leave a few small chunks.

2 Whip the double cream in a mixing bowl with an electric hand whisk until stiff peaks form.

3 In another bowl, mix the condensed milk with the lemon juice, vanilla extract and strawberries until well combined, then gently fold in the whipped cream.

4 Pour the mixture into a loaf tin or any freezer-safe container. Smooth the top with a spatula, cover and freeze for at least 6 hours, or overnight, until the ice cream is firm.

5 Remove from the freezer for 10 minutes to soften a little before serving.

If the strawberries are very sweet, you might not need the sugar, as the condensed milk is already pretty sweet.

You can add a few drops of red food colouring at the same time as the lemon juice if you want a stronger pink colour.

CHOC-CHIP BANANA LOAF

Not sure what to do with your over-ripe bananas? Why not try my delicious banana loaf? This is a massive hit at home, served with a nice cup of tea.

SERVES 6–8

3 ripe bananas
125g (4½oz) unsalted
    butter, melted
125g (4½oz) golden caster
    sugar
2 tablespoons maple syrup
1 teaspoon vanilla extract
2 eggs, beaten
175g (6oz) plain flour
1 teaspoon baking powder
½ teaspoon ground
    cinnamon
50g (1¾oz) chocolate chips

1 Preheat the oven to 180°C (400°F), Gas Mark 6. Mash 2 of the bananas with a fork until smooth. This is a fun job the kids could do.

2 Place the melted butter, sugar, maple syrup, vanilla extract, eggs, flour and baking powder in a large bowl. Mix well to make a smooth cake batter.

3 Add the mashed banana, cinnamon and chocolate chips. Mix again until well combined.

4 Line a loaf tin with baking paper, leaving it to overhang the sides of the tin to help remove the loaf when cooked. Pour the cake mixture into the tin.

5 Slice the remaining banana in half lengthways and place on top of the batter. Bake in the oven for 45 minutes –1 hour, until well risen and bouncy to the touch. You can check it's done by poking a skewer or knife into the centre – if it comes out clean, it's ready to serve.

If you prefer, swap the chocolate chips for raisins, chopped nuts, or both.

PUFF PASTRY APPLE RINGS

These pastry-covered apple rings, scented with warming cinnamon, are a fun take on apple pie. Delicious hot from the oven as a hand-held dessert, or perfect for lunchboxes and picnics.

MAKES 5

-

1 large apple

1–2 teaspoons ground cinnamon

5 teaspoons granulated sugar

160g (5¾oz) ready-rolled puff pastry (½ a sheet)

1 egg, beaten

1 Preheat the oven to 180°C (400°F), Gas Mark 6. Cut the apple horizontally into 5 chunky slices, then remove the cores with a small pastry cutter to make the slices into rings.

2 Mix the cinnamon and sugar together in a shallow bowl and coat the apple rings generously with the mixture, ensuring both sides are covered.

3 Unroll the puff pastry and cut it into long, thin strips. Wrap the pastry strips around the apple rings, spiralling in and out until each ring is fully covered. Place on a baking tray lined with baking paper.

4 Brush the pastry-covered apple slices with the beaten egg to give them a golden shine.

5 Sprinkle any remaining cinnamon sugar over the pastry and cook in the oven for 15–20 minutes, until the pastry is puffed and golden brown.

FUN WITH FRUIT & VEG

Getting kids excited about eating their veggies and fruit can be a challenge – trust me, I know. But it doesn't have to be. This chapter is all about making healthy food fun and interactive for little hands. Here, you'll find creative ideas that will have your kids eager to help in the kitchen. From vegetable cars and orange butterflies to crunchy chickpeas for a tasty snack, these recipes turn everyday produce into playful and delicious creations. Roll up your sleeves, get the kids involved and let's have some fun while making mealtimes more colourful and nutritious!

STRAWBERRY ROSE

A super-pretty rose you can eat! This one takes a little practice but once you get the hang of it, it's easy. We use these as cake decorations, on fruit platters and for special occasions such as Valentine's Day – make several for a little bouquet.

MAKES 1
-
1 firm ripe strawberry, hulled

1 Insert a skewer about one-third of the way into the strawberry's stem end. Use a sharp knife to make a cut down into the side of the strawberry to make a lower petal. Repeat to make 4 or 5 petals around the base.

2 Now make another ring of petals a little way further up the strawberry, this time making the cuts a little deeper than before, allowing the petals to curl back slightly.

3 Continue making rings of petals around the strawberry to the top. Carefully pull back the layers of the strawberry with your fingers to help the petals open up.

ORANGE BUTTERFLY

I have been making these cute oranges while working with kids for years, and they're a favourite in the summer.

MAKES 4
-
1 orange, cut into quarters

1 Make a cut down the middle of one of the orange quarters, stopping about halfway. Now slide the knife between the flesh and the skin, again stopping halfway.

2 Make a smaller cut down the middle of the orange segment from the other end.

3 Carefully open the segment – you'll see a butterfly! Repeat with the remaining orange quarters.

POTATO FUNNY FACES

My boys and I love creating fun potato characters using pieces of vegetable, pepperoni, olives, cheese or anything else we find in the refrigerator. Serve them with butter, cheese, tuna mayo or baked beans. This is a great way to get kids involved and try new vegetables. See who can make the funniest face!

MR PEPPERONI POTATO

1 broccoli floret, cooked
1 slice of pepperoni
2 slices of stuffed green olive

SILLY BIRD MAN

2 green beans, cooked
1 chunk of red pepper
2 slices of stuffed black olive

Use potatoes of any size and bake or boil them whole in their skins.

Use a skewer or knife to make holes or slits in the potatoes to insert the other ingredients.

APPLE MONSTERS

These delicious apple bites are great fun to make. And with peanut butter, strawberry and seeds, they're a healthy little snack.

MAKES 4

-

1 apple, quartered and
    cored
2 teaspoons peanut
    butter
4 slices of strawberry
edible eye cake
    decorations
handful of sunflower or
    pumpkin seeds

1 Cut a wedge out of the skin side of each apple quarter to create a mouth, and spread a thin layer of peanut butter inside each mouth.

2 Place a strawberry slice in the centre of each mouth to resemble a tongue sticking out. For the teeth, make a line of seeds along the top edge of each mouth, sticking them into the peanut butter.

3 Spread a dot of peanut butter on the backs of the edible eyes and stick them to the monsters!

Try swapping the peanut butter for chocolate or Biscoff spread, and the seeds for mini marshmallows, to create different monsters. Chocolate chips make great eyes, too.

MANGO & COCONUT CLUSTERS

A delicious, sweet and fruity snack or dessert idea – perfect as a refreshing treat.

MAKES 6

-

2 ripe mangos, peeled and diced

225ml (8fl oz) coconut yogurt

1–2 tablespoons honey

200g (7oz) white chocolate, melted and stirred well

Instead of completely coating the clusters, you could just drizzle a little melted chocolate over them instead. It will set immediately.

1 Place the mango and yogurt in a bowl, mix together and sweeten to taste with honey.

2 Spoon mounds of the mixture onto a baking tray lined with baking paper. Freeze until firm.

3 Coat the mango clusters in the melted white chocolate and return to the freezer until the chocolate is firm.

CRUNCHY CARS

With a little creativity, you can transform simple vegetables into crunchy mini cars that are as fun to make as they are to eat. These vegetable cars will zoom right into your children's mouths!

MAKES 6

-

3 baby peppers
1 cucumber, thickly sliced
Easy Hummus (see page
 169)
6 slices of cherry tomato
thin carrot sticks (optional)

1 Cut the peppers in half lengthways and remove the seeds and stems.

2 Insert 4 short lengths of toothpick into the sides of the peppers to hold the wheels.

3 Push a slice of cucumber onto each piece of toothpick.

4 Fill the pepper cars with hummus and place a slice of cherry tomato at the front of each as a steering wheel. Insert carrot sticks at the backs of the cars if you like.

Get the children to create their own car designs using other fruit and veg – think radishes, apples, pears or beetroot cut into different shapes.

WATERMELON PIZZA

This is both a fun way to serve fruit and a delicious and refreshing pudding. The kids can cut the fruit into different shapes and use their imagination to pretend they are making pizza!

Try different fruits as pizza toppings to see how realistic you can make it.

SERVES 4

-

1 thick slice of watermelon

6 tablespoons yogurt of your choice

handful of blueberries

handful of raspberries

a few strawberries, chopped

desiccated coconut, for sprinkling

1 Lay the slice of melon on a board and cut into quarters.

2 Spread the yogurt over the melon as you would tomato sauce on a pizza.

3 Arrange the fruit on top of the yogurt like toppings on the pizza.

4 Sprinkle the pizza with desiccated coconut to resemble grated cheese.

5 Separate the slices a little to make it easier to serve.

BANANA DOLPHINS

This idea is so simple but it will definitely make your children smile! I make these at breakfast to set the mood for the day.

MAKES 2
-
2 bananas, halved
2 blueberries

Use the other halves of the bananas to make the Frozen Banana Pops opposite, or simply slice them over porridge or cereal.

1 Lay the banana halves on their sides and cut a slit through the stalks, into the tops of the bananas.

2 Push a blueberry into each dolphin mouth to hold them open.

3 Use a pen to draw an eye on each side of each banana to bring the dolphins to life.

FROZEN BANANA POPS

I often make these creamy banana lollies at lunchtime to serve as an after-school snack or a sweet treat after dinner.

MAKES 4

-

2 bananas, peeled and
  halved
100–150ml (3½–5½fl oz)
  yogurt of your choice

TO DECORATE
sprinkles
dried fruit
nuts
chocolate chips
edible eye cake
  decorations

1 Insert a lolly stick into the cut end of each banana half and place on a baking tray lined with baking paper.

2 Dip the bananas into the yogurt, making sure they are well coated.

3 Decorate the lollies with your choice of decorations, then freeze for at least 3 hours, until completely solid.

BUG SNACKS

~~~~~~

Packed with fresh veggies and added cuteness, these adorable snacks are always a hit. Perfect for spring and summer holidays, you can let the children make these on play dates and afternoons at home!

MAKES 6

-

4 tablespoons cream
  cheese
3 baby cucumbers,
  halved lengthwise,
  plus a few extra slices
12 cherry tomatoes,
  halved
a few chives
edible eye cake
  decorations
basil leaves or salad
  leaves, to decorate

Use Easy Hummus (see page 169) instead of the cream cheese if you prefer.

1 Spread most of the cream cheese over the cut sides of the cucumber halves.

2 Arrange the halved cherry tomatoes on top, cut sides down.

3 Cut the chives into shorter lengths and poke into the cream cheese to stick up like antennae.

4 Spread a dot of cream cheese on the back of each edible eye and stick in place.

5 Halve a few small slices of cucumber and press into the cream cheese as little wings.

6 Arrange the bugs on a plate or board with a few basil leaves or salad leaves scattered around for a garden-like effect.

SOUR PATCH GRAPES

Looking for a deliciously healthy snack that satisfies your sweet tooth? Try my sour patch grapes! This simple yet irresistible treat combines the natural sweetness of grapes with a tangy twist, making it a perfect alternative to traditional sugary snacks.

SERVES 4
-
450g (1lb) seedless green grapes
juice of 1–2 limes
23g (¾oz) sachet of sugar-free orange jelly powder
23g (¾oz) sachet of sugar-free raspberry jelly powder
23g (¾oz) sachet of sugar-free blackcurrant jelly powder

If your children are very young, cut the grapes in half to avoid the risk of choking.

1 Place the grapes in a bowl with the lime juice and toss gently to coat evenly. Set aside for 5 minutes.

2 Pour the jelly powders into 3 separate bowls. Add a few grapes to each bowl and gently shake the bowls to coat the grapes.

3 Place the grapes on a baking tray lined with baking paper and repeat with the remaining grapes. Freeze for 2–3 hours, until firm.

CRISPY CHICKPEAS

Enjoy these crispy, crunchy chickpeas as a snack, in lunchboxes or sprinkled over salads and soups for added texture.

SERVES 4
-
400g (14oz) can chickpeas, drained and rinsed, then patted dry with kitchen paper
2–3 tablespoons olive or vegetable oil
1 teaspoon paprika
1 teaspoon garlic granules
1 teaspoon ground cumin
pinch of ground turmeric
salt and pepper

These chickpeas could also be cooked in an air fryer. Spread them out in the air fryer basket and shake regularly during cooking so they crisp evenly.

1 Preheat the air fryer to 200°C or the oven to 200°C (425°F), Gas Mark 7. Place the chickpeas in a bowl and toss with the oil, spices and some salt and pepper.

2 Spread them out on a baking tray lined with baking paper and cook in the air fryer or oven for 25–40 minutes, shaking halfway through.

3 The chickpeas are ready when they are golden and crispy. Let them cool slightly – they will continue to crisp up as they cool down.

APPLE & YOGURT PARTY RINGS

These colourful and healthy rings will quickly become your family's new favourite snactivity!

MAKES 5

-

1 large red apple
5 tablespoons yogurt of
  your choice

TO DECORATE
sprinkles
white chocolate chips
blueberries

1 Place the apple on a board and cut horizontally in 5 chunky slices.

2 Use a small cookie cutter to remove the cores and make the slices into rings.

3 Spread the tops of the apple rings with yogurt until evenly coated.

4 Decorate the apple rings with your choice of toppings. Everyone can do their own!

Get creative with your toppings – chocolate shavings, fudge chunks, raspberries and chopped nuts work well, too.

In warm weather, pop the apple rings into the freezer for 2–3 hours for a frozen treat.

HOLIDAY HELPERS

Holidays and special occasions always seem to arrive in the blink of an eye, and with them comes the perfect opportunity to get creative in the kitchen! This chapter is filled with holiday-inspired recipes that will encourage kids to get involved in cooking. Whether it's Easter, Valentine's Day, Fireworks Night, Eid, Diwali, Christmas, Halloween or any other special occasion, there's a fun and festive dish waiting to be created. These recipes aren't just about food, they're about making lasting memories with your family while exploring new flavours and traditions in the kitchen. Let the holiday cooking adventures begin!

TORTILLA SNACTIVITY

Recreated by so many of my followers, this is definitely a beloved holiday favourite! The idea is to sandwich together two soft flour tortillas with fillings, the top tortilla with fun shapes cut out of it. They are then baked to make a crispy, melty morsel.

EASTER CARROTS

Use a carrot-shaped cutter for the holes. Spread the bottom tortilla with tomato sauce and add grated Red Leicester cheese and basil leaves as the carrot leaves.

Once your creation is ready, give it a light spray of oil or a brush of butter, then bake it in the oven at 200°C (425°F), Gas Mark 7, for 5–10 minutes until crispy.

VALENTINE'S HEARTS

Use a heart-shaped cutter for the holes. Spread the bottom tortilla with tomato sauce and add grated Cheddar and pepperoni slices for a pinky-red colour.

CHRISTMAS RUDOLPH

Use a gingerbread man-shaped cutter upside down. Spread the bottom tortilla with peanut butter and add white chocolate buttons, red Smarties or Skittles and edible eye cake decorations.

CHRISTMAS TREES

Use a Christmas tree-shaped cutter for the holes. Spread the bottom tortilla with tomato sauce, add grated Cheddar and dried oregano, then stars cut from a carrot or orange pepper.

EID STARS & MOONS

Use a star-shaped cutter and create the moons free-hand with scissors. Spread the bottom tortilla with tomato sauce and add grated Cheddar.

DIWALI FIREWORKS

Use a star-shaped cutter for the fireworks and add tails free-hand with scissors. Spread the bottom tortilla with tomato sauce and top with grated Red Leicester cheese.

HALLOWEEN PUMPKIN

Use a knife to carve a spooky face out of the top tortilla. Spread the bottom tortilla with tomato sauce, then grated Red Leicester cheese and a basil leaf for the stem.

CHOCOLATE DRIZZLE ART

Keep the kids engaged with fun, creative and edible art! Melted chocolate can be coloured with a touch of food colouring. Add a few other ingredients and you have some awesome decorative treats for a whole host of different celebrations.

1 Melt your chocolate (white, milk or dark) in a microwavable bowl in the microwave for 60–90 seconds, stirring regularly, until runny. Add a few drops of gel food colouring, if desired, and mix well.

2 Transfer the melted chocolate to a piping bag. Cut a tiny hole at the pointed end of the piping bag and test the flow, enlarging the hole if necessary. Then get creative!

SNOWMAN

Dip a pretzel stick into melted white chocolate and stick 3 giant white chocolate buttons on it. Use the chocolate as glue to stick pretzel arms on the back, chocolate chips for buttons, an orange Smartie for the nose and edible eyes.

HEART

Lay a chocolate-covered stick biscuit on baking paper and drizzle melted white chocolate mixed with red food colouring over it to create a heart. Decorate with sprinkles.

CHRISTMAS TREE

Lay a small chocolate bar for a trunk on baking paper and drizzle melted white chocolate mixed with green food colouring over it for branches. Decorate with sprinkles and a chocolate star.

GHOST

Lay a wooden lolly stick on baking paper and spoon melted white chocolate over it in the shape of a ghost. Add eyes and a mouth with milk chocolate buttons.

BUNNY

Lay a white chocolate finger biscuit on baking paper and drizzle melted white chocolate over it in a bunny shape. Top with a mini egg.

SPIDER WEB

Break pretzel sticks into short lengths and arrange 8 pieces on baking paper like the spokes of a wheel. Drizzle melted white chocolate over the top to create the web, then decorate with sprinkles.

FLUFFY CREAM FLOATS

Create these fun, festive whipped cream floats for Valentine's Day, Christmas or Halloween. Whipped cream holds up surprisingly well when frozen and these adorable floats can be kept in the freezer for up to a month. Whip them out of the freezer to make any hot drink feel extra special for the holidays!

Simply use a can of squirty cream to create fun shapes on baking paper and top with decorations and sprinkles. Transfer to the freezer for 1–2 hours, or until firm enough to peel off the paper. Store in a freezer bag in the freezer until ready to use in hot chocolate or coffee.

HEART

Spray a heart shape and top with mini marshmallows and colourful sprinkles for a sweet touch.

GHOST

Spray a blob shape with a wavy bottom. Stick on edible eye cake decorations and a line of chocolate chips for the mouth of this cute little ghost.

SNOWMAN

Spray a large blob for the body and a smaller blob for the head. Add edible eyes, an orange Smartie for the nose and chocolate chips for buttons.

DIWALI FIREWORK SKEWERS

These colourful fruit skewers are so fun to make and kids love them. Perfect for a snack or as a fun addition to any party.

MAKES 3
-
3 fingers of mango
12 blueberries
6 green grapes
3 red grapes
3 chunks of banana
3 large strawberries, hulled

1 Start by cutting a V-shaped wedge out of one end of each mango finger. Thread the mango pieces onto 3 wooden skewers.

2 Next thread on the blueberries and grapes, alternating the colours to create a vibrant and delicious rainbow of flavours.

3 Add a chunk of banana to each skewer, then finish with a strawberry to make the top of each rocket.

Gather together a host of different colourful fruits to make these firework skewers. Try cherries, raspberries, blackberries, fingers of melon or chunks of persimmon, too.

EGG & TOAST FUN

Egg and toast are classic comfort foods that never disappoint, but with a little creativity, they can be transformed into something special for the holidays. Here's how to make breakfast extra festive!

SERVES 1
-
1 egg
1 tablespoon butter
1 slice of bread

TO DECORATE
chilli flakes
black sesame seeds
black olives
basil leaves
slices of chorizo
slices of cheese
chives

1 Separate the egg white from the egg yolk and place in 2 separate bowls. Melt the butter in a nonstick frying pan over a medium-high heat. While the butter melts, use cookie cutters to cut fun shapes out of your sliced bread.

2 Place the slice of bread in the pan and fry until the underside is crispy and golden. Flip over the bread and pour the egg white into one hole and the yolk into the other. Fry until the egg is fully cooked, covering with a lid if required.

3 Season the egg and decorate with whatever ingredients you need to create your characters.

You can toast the cut-out pieces of bread and spread with butter, jam or peanut butter for an extra treat.

HEART

Use a heart-shaped cutter in the centre of the bread. Crack in and season a whole egg while frying the bread. Cut a heart shape from a chorizo slice and add alongside.

EASTER CHICK

Fry an egg and place on top of a piece of buttered toast. Use black sesame seeds to make the eyes and cut small pieces out of a slice of cheese for the beak and feet.

PUMPKIN & GHOST

Use a ghost- and a pumpkin-shaped cutter to create the holes in the bread. Pour the egg white into the ghost hole and the yolk into the pumpkin hole while frying the bread. Decorate with pieces of black olive and a basil leaf.

SNOWMAN & STARS

Use a snowman- and a star-shaped cutter to create the holes in the bread. Pour the egg white into the snowman hole and the yolk into the star holes while frying the bread. Decorate with black olives, a cheese nose and chorizo scarf.

EASTER BUNNY & CHICK

Use a bunny- and a chick-shaped cutter to create the holes in the bread. Pour the egg white into the bunny hole and the yolk into the chick hole while frying the bread. Decorate with black sesame-seed eyes and chive whiskers.

HALLOWEEN BURGERS

Every Halloween half term, it's our tradition to have burgers. But here's the fun idea – we grab some cheese slices and a small knife and get creative. We carve out eerie faces in the cheese and place them right on top of our burgers for a spooky treat that's as fun to make as it is to eat!

Place the cheese slices on the burgers after cooking, or place them on top while the burgers are in the pan if you like them more melted.

Let everyone make their own pumpkin face and place it on top of their burger.

PUKING PUMPKIN

Halloween pumpkins often get neglected in the garden, so why not keep them inside where they can really be appreciated? Even better, turn them into a gruesome yet delicious centrepiece – spooky, fun and a hit at any party!

SERVES 8–10
-
1 large Halloween pumpkin
3 avocados, peeled and pitted
juice of 1 lime
1 teaspoon paprika
1 teaspoon garlic granules
1 teaspoon chilli flakes (optional)
1 red onion, finely chopped
½–1 teaspoon ground cumin
salt and pepper
tortilla chips, to serve

1 Scoop out the pumpkin and cut a mouth big enough to fill with the guacamole.

2 Place the remaining ingredients except the tortilla chips in a mixing bowl. Mash with a fork to make a smoothish paste. Season with salt, pepper and cumin to taste. Serve on a platter with the carved pumpkin, surrounded by tortilla chips for scooping.

Try squirming worms – aka spaghetti in sauce – tumbling out the mouth for a creepy alternative.

MINI ROLL MADNESS

Are you ready to unleash your creativity? Turn a simple pack of chocolate mini rolls into something extraordinary. Mini rolls are the perfect building blocks to help bring your ideas to life. And the best bit? You get to eat your art!

MOTOR CAR

Stick on 4 white chocolate buttons for wheels using melted chocolate for glue. Decorate the rest of the car using Smarties, colourful sweets like gummy bears, chocolate chips or even fruit pieces for headlights, windows and decoration. It's a fun, sweet activity perfect for any car lover.

GIANT SPIDER

Use 8 pretzel sticks or chocolate-covered stick biscuits for the legs. Snap them in half and stick back together at an angle using melted chocolate, then poke them into the sides of a mini roll. Stick on 2 edible eye cake decorations with melted chocolate or create your own with chocolate chips or white chocolate buttons.

RUDOLPH THE REINDEER

Insert 4 lengths of pretzel stick underneath a mini roll for legs and check Rudolph stands up. Use a white chocolate button for his face, 2 edible eye cake decorations and a Smartie nose, and stick them on with melted chocolate. Finish with pieces of curvy pretzel as antlers.

FESTIVE CHOCOLATE FUN

Children love Christmas and they love chocolate, so why not put the two together and give them something to do with those little hands while they wait for the big day to arrive? Here are some perfect festive snacks to share with little ones, adding a fun and tasty touch to any Christmas celebration.

Melt the chocolate in a heatproof bowl in the microwave on full power, checking and stirring regularly, until it's runny.

Get creative – add any other fun ingredients you like to make your bark unique. Think nuts, dried fruit or popcorn.

RUDOLPH BREADSTICKS

Children love breadsticks, and these adorable bundles are sure to make them smile. Melt some milk or dark chocolate and break some long breadsticks in half. Holding 2 pieces of breadstick together, dip the broken ends about a third of the way up in the melted chocolate, let the excess drip off, then place on baking paper. Add red Smarties for noses, and edible eyes, then let the chocolate harden in the refrigerator.

MINI BISCUIT HOUSE

If you're craving the fun of building a gingerbread house but don't want to spend too much money or deal with the stress of making it from scratch, here's a quick, affordable and super-fun alternative! Simply stick 3 rectangular biscuits together with melted white chocolate and decorate the roof with sweeties.

CHRISTMAS CHOCOLATE BARK

This lovely chocolate bark is a fun combination of sweet and salty, and it's fully customizable, limited only by what you have in the cupboard and your imagination! Melt your chocolate and spread on a sheet of baking paper in an even layer, then have fun with sweeties, sprinkles and pretzels. Harden in the refrigerator for 1–2 hours.

LEFTOVER INSPIRATION

One of my favourite ways to get creative in the kitchen is by transforming leftovers into something new and exciting. This section is all about taking those food scraps and forgotten bits and turning them into tasty snacks or reinventing old meals into something fresh. Whether it's using up extra veggies, turning last night's roast into tasty taquitos or creating unexpected treats from what's left behind, these recipes are perfect for minimizing food waste while adding new flavours to your meals. I love making the most of what I've got, and I hope these ideas inspire you to do the same – no waste, just great taste!

POTATO PEEL CRISPS

Ever wondered what to do with potato peelings rather than tossing them out? Turn them into crispy, flavourful and waste-free snacks that are packed with flavour!

SERVES 2
-
peel from 4 large potatoes, rinsed under cold water and patted dry with a clean towel

1–2 tablespoons vegetable oil

1–2 teaspoons seasoning of your choice (I use peri peri)

salt and pepper

dipping sauce (I use sweet chilli), to serve (optional)

1 Preheat the air fryer to 180°C, or the oven to 180°C (400°F), Gas Mark 6.

2 Place the peelings in a large mixing bowl with the oil, your chosen seasoning, and salt and pepper to taste. Mix well to ensure all the skins are evenly seasoned.

3 Spread in a single layer in the air fryer basket or on a baking tray. You may want to line the tray with baking paper for an easy clean up.

4 Bake in the air fryer or oven for 10–15 minutes, until the potato peelings are golden and crispy. Be sure to check halfway through and toss the skins for even crispiness. Let them cool for a few minutes before tucking in.

I used peri peri seasoning here, but there are plenty of other spice blends available. Or just go for a simple sprinkle of salt.

HOMEMADE TORTILLA CHIPS

This is a great idea for using up all the cut-out shapes from my Tortilla Snactivity (see page 142). Homemade tortilla chips are simple to make and you can serve them with dips or make loaded nachos. I love this simple and effective recipe – no waste and super-affordable.

This recipe is very flexible. Just adjust the amount of oil and seasoning depending on the amount of tortilla offcuts you have.

SERVES 2
-
50g (1¾oz) leftover soft flour tortilla pieces
½ tablespoon vegetable oil or melted butter
½ teaspoon Cajun seasoning
dips, to serve

1 Preheat the air fryer to 180°C, or the oven to 180°C (400°F), Gas Mark 6. Lay the tortilla shapes out on a board and brush with the oil or melted butter. Sprinkle with the seasoning and season with salt and pepper.

2 Spread in a single layer in the air fryer basket or on a baking tray. You may want to line the tray with baking paper for an easy clean up.

3 Bake for 4–6 minutes in the air fryer or 4–7 minutes in the oven, until golden and crispy. Serve with dips.

Try making sweet tortilla chips if you prefer. Mix some ground cinnamon in a bowl with some caster sugar, then use the mixture to sprinkle on the chips before cooking, instead of the Cajun seasoning.

CHOCOLATE SALAMI

~~~~~~~

This fun, no-bake dessert is perfect for using up leftover chocolate, especially after holidays like Easter and Christmas when you may have an excess of sweet treats. Serve your chocolate salami as a delicious treat for guests or family, or keep it for yourself to enjoy with a cup of coffee or tea.

SERVES 6–8

-

400g (14oz) leftover chocolate – dark, milk or a mix

1 tablespoon butter

100g (3½oz) digestive or other plain biscuits, broken into pieces

50g (1¾oz) Smarties

50g (1¾oz) whole pistachios

50g (1¾oz) mixed hazelnuts, almonds and walnuts

50g (1¾oz) dried fruit

50g (1¾oz) mini marshmallows (optional)

1 Break the chocolate into pieces and place it in a microwavable bowl with the butter. Melt in the microwave in 30-second bursts, stirring in between, until it is runny. Stir the remaining ingredients into the chocolate until everything is well coated.

2 Pour the chocolate mixture onto a sheet of baking paper and use a spatula to form it into a salami-like shape. Roll the mixture tightly in the baking paper, twisting the ends like a sweet wrapper to secure it.

3 Place the rolled chocolate salami in the refrigerator to chill for at least 3 hours, or until firm. Once set, remove it from the refrigerator and carefully slice into rounds, just like you would a real salami.

This recipe is hugely versatile, so feel free to adjust the ingredients based on what you have available. You can add other sweets and chocolate shapes, different nuts or dried fruits (raisins, sultanas, cherries or cranberries) to personalize it.

GARLIC BREAD CRUSTS

Don't throw away your bread crusts – make my tasty garlic bread crusts instead! So many of us cut off the crusts and throw them away and it's such a waste. When the boys were younger, they didn't even realize they were eating leftover crusts, they used to snaffle these up in seconds. Share them with the kids or save them for yourself as cook's perks.

You can experiment with the flavours here, trying out just about any spices and dried herbs you like.

SERVES 2
-
leftover crusts from 4 slices of bread
1 tablespoon melted butter
1 tablespoon grated Parmesan cheese
1 teaspoon crushed garlic or garlic granules
½ teaspoon dried oregano
salt and pepper

1 Preheat the air fryer to 200°C, or the oven to 200°C (425°F), Gas Mark 7. Place the crusts in a mixing bowl and drizzle with the melted butter. Add all the remaining ingredients and toss the crusts until evenly coated.

2 Spread in a single layer in the air fryer basket or on a baking tray. You may want to line the tray with baking paper for an easy clean up.

3 Bake in the air fryer or oven for 5–7 minutes, until golden and crispy.

These crusts make great croûtons if you chop them into smaller pieces. Serve as a topping for your favourite soup, salad or pasta dish.

VEGGIE TOTS

We've all been there – random vegetables piling up in the kitchen, and no idea what to do with them. Instead of letting them go to waste, try my delicious veggie tots. They're the perfect solution, especially if you've got leftover boiled potatoes, too. This is a simple way to avoid food waste.

SERVES 4

-

1 courgette, grated

1 carrot, grated

1 large baking potato, boiled
   and mashed

100g (3½oz) Cheddar cheese,
   grated

2 large eggs, beaten

1 teaspoon garlic granules

1 teaspoon all-purpose
   seasoning

1 teaspoon dried mixed herbs

1 teaspoon paprika

vegetable oil, for frying
   (optional)

salt and pepper

1 Place all the ingredients in a large bowl, season to taste and mix everything together until well combined. Take small portions of the mixture in your hands and roll them into small balls, about the size of a golf ball.

2 There are 2 options for cooking these veggie tots – either oven baking or shallow frying. If baking in the oven, preheat the oven to 200°C (425°F), Gas Mark 7. Place the tots on a baking tray lined with baking paper, ensuring they are not touching. Cook in the oven for 20–25 minutes, or until golden and crispy, flipping halfway through.

3 If frying, heat a little vegetable oil in a frying pan over a medium heat and gently place the tots into the pan. Cook for 3–4 minutes on each side, until golden brown.

ROAST DINNER 'TAQUITOS'

Here's how to use up your leftovers after a roast dinner. These tasty treats are inspired by Mexican taquitos and are perfect as lunchbox fillers, or just to have for dinner the next day.

SERVES 4

-

8 mini soft flour tortillas

8 slices of leftover roast meat

4 leftover roast potatoes

**leftover cooked vegetables,
    such as carrots, parsnips,
    sprouts or broccoli**

**small handful of grated
    cheese (optional)**

**8 tablespoons gravy, plus
    extra for dipping**

1 Preheat the air fryer to 200°C, or the oven to 200°C (425°F), Gas Mark 7. Lay the tortillas out on a board. Cut the meat, potatoes and vegetables into small pieces and divide between the tortillas. Sprinkle with grated cheese, if using, then roll up the tortillas tightly.

2 Place the gravy in a shallow bowl and roll the tortillas in it to coat them on all sides. Place in the air fryer basket or on a baking tray lined with baking paper and cook in the air fryer or oven for about 10 minutes, until crispy on the outside and piping hot inside. Serve with extra delicious gravy for dipping.

STUFFED YORKSHIRE PUDS

If you have too many Yorkshire puddings in the refrigerator or freezer and don't know what to do with them, why not turn them into something new? Stuffing your Yorkshires can breathe new life into them, whether you're using leftovers or just looking to try something new. Here are a few mouth-watering ideas to inspire you.

FULL ENGLISH BREAKFAST

For a hearty twist, fill your Yorkshires with a full English breakfast! Add crispy bacon, cooked sausage, scrambled eggs, baked beans, grilled tomato and mushrooms for a filling and delicious brunch.

Cook your Yorkshire puddings according to packet instructions or simply reheat, then try some of these filling suggestions, or create your own favourites.

BEANS & CHEESE

For a quick and satisfying snack, fill your Yorkshire puddings with baked beans, top with grated cheese and return to the oven until melted. The warm, gooey cheese pairs perfectly with the soft beans.

SHEPHERD'S PIE

Stuff your Yorkshire puddings with leftover savoury minced beef. Add a few tablespoons of peas and a dollop of creamy mashed potatoes on top for a deliciously comforting meal.

CAMEMBERT & HONEY

Cheese is the perfect filling for a Yorkshire pudding. My favourite is a wedge of camembert topped with honey, rosemary and chilli flakes. Bake until the cheese melts into a gooey, molten pool. Break up another Yorkshire pudding to dip in the melted cheese!

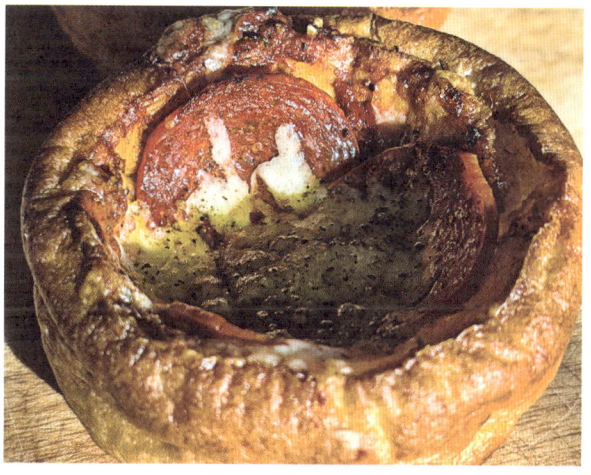

PIZZA-STYLE YORKIES

Transform your Yorkshire puddings into mini pizzas! Spread with tomato sauce, sprinkle over some cheese and top with pepperoni or your favourite pizza toppings. Return to the oven until the cheese is bubbly and golden.

BASE RECIPES

Every great meal starts with a solid foundation and this chapter is all about those essential base recipes for the dishes that can be found in this book. These are the go-to staples that set the stage for countless dishes, from sauces to salads and sides. Once you have these basic recipes in your back pocket, you'll be able to build and customize them into a wide range of meals, adding your own spin and creativity.

RED SAUCE

A delicious recipe for a hidden-vegetable tomato sauce for pasta and pizza bases – perfect for my Tortilla Snactivity on page 142. You can make a big batch of this and freeze it in an ice cube tray, ready for when you need it.

**MAKES ENOUGH FOR
3–4 SERVINGS**
-
2 tablespoons olive oil
1 onion, finely chopped
2 garlic cloves, crushed
1 red pepper, cored,
   deseeded and finely
   chopped
1 small courgette, finely
   chopped
1 carrot, finely chopped
400g (14oz) can chopped
   tomatoes or 6–8 fresh
   tomatoes
1 tablespoon tomato purée
   (optional)
1 teaspoon dried oregano
1 teaspoon dried or chopped
   fresh basil
½ teaspoon sugar (optional)
salt and pepper

1 In a large pan, heat the olive oil over a medium heat. Add the onion, garlic and red pepper, and sauté for 5–7 minutes, until softened. Stir in the grated courgette and carrot, and cook for 10–15 minutes, stirring regularly, until the vegetables soften.

2 Stir in the tomatoes, tomato purée, if using, and herbs, and season with salt and pepper. Bring the sauce to a simmer and cook for 15–20 minutes, adding a splash of water if it gets too dry, until thickened.

3 Allow to cool, then blend the sauce in a blender until smooth. Adjust the seasoning to taste, adding the sugar if you feel it's needed.

4 Store the sauce in an airtight jar in the refrigerator for up to 5 days. Alternatively, chill overnight in the refrigerator, then transfer to an airtight container or ice cube trays and freeze for up to 3 months.

The optional tomato purée will give the sauce a deeper flavour, while the sugar will balance out the acidity. For a richer, deeper flavour, you can add ground cumin, paprika or chilli flakes to taste.

GREEN SAUCE

My take on pesto is a great way to hide some vegetables in your children's meal. Use it in place of tomato sauce in tortillas, on pasta and even on pizzas. I freeze leftovers in an ice cube tray, then warm up a cube or two with a little of the pasta-cooking water and toss it with spaghetti for a quick and tasty meal. The amount you add to your pasta is totally up to you – I guess it depends how green you want it!

SERVES 6–8

-

50g (1¾oz) basil leaves

30g (1oz) spinach leaves

30g (1oz) pine nuts or walnuts

2 garlic cloves, peeled

50g (1¾oz) Parmesan cheese, grated

¼ teaspoon salt

125ml (4fl oz) extra-virgin olive oil, plus extra for storing

lemon juice (optional)

pepper

1 Place the basil, spinach, pine nuts or walnuts, garlic, Parmesan, salt and black pepper to taste in a food processor. Pulse a few times until everything is roughly chopped.

2 With the processor running, gradually add the olive oil in a steady stream until the pesto is smooth and well combined. Taste and adjust the seasoning with more salt, pepper or lemon juice if desired.

3 Store the pesto in a jar with a thin layer of olive oil on top to prevent oxidation. It will keep for up to 7 days in the refrigerator. Alternatively, freeze any leftovers in an airtight container or ice cube tray for up to 3 months. Thaw in the refrigerator overnight before use and stir in a little extra olive oil if it seems too thick.

If you like a brighter flavour, add 1–2 tablespoons of lemon juice to the pesto. You could also add more veg to the blender to make it super-healthy – a handful of cooked broccoli works well.

MY SPECIAL SALAD

A colourful, crunchy and delicious treat. Packed with fresh veggies, tasty toppings and a hint of sweetness, this salad is perfect for families who want to enjoy healthy, fun meals together. Whether you're eating it at the dinner table or out and about on a picnic, this salad is sure to bring smiles with every bite.

SERVES 4

-

100g (3½oz) sweetcorn

1 head of romaine or iceberg lettuce, chopped

½ cucumber, sliced

1 tomato, chopped

1 carrot, grated or julienned

½ small red onion, finely sliced

½ celery stick, chopped

½ orange pepper, cored, deseeded and diced

DRESSING

2 tablespoons olive oil

1 tablespoon white wine vinegar

½ tablespoon honey

½ teaspoon Dijon mustard

1 tablespoon lemon juice

1 tablespoon mayonnaise (optional)

1 tablespoon Parmesan cheese, grated (optional)

salt and pepper

1 Place all the salad ingredients in a large bowl and toss together. In a small bowl, whisk together the dressing ingredients until smooth.

2 Drizzle the tangy-sweet dressing over the salad and toss gently to coat, or serve the dressing on the side so everyone can add as much as they like.

EASY HUMMUS

This creamy hummus is perfect for anyone looking to whip up a quick and delicious snack. With just a few storecupboard items like chickpeas, tahini, lemon juice and olive oil, you can create a smooth and flavourful dip that's great for veggies, pitta or even spreading on sandwiches. It's so easy, you'll wonder why you haven't made it sooner.

SERVES 4
-
**400g (14oz) can chickpeas,
   drained and rinsed
3 tablespoons tahini
2 tablespoons olive oil
juice of 1 lemon
2 garlic cloves, peeled
1 teaspoon ground cumin
   (optional)
1 teaspoon paprika (optional)
salt**

1 Place all the ingredients in a blender and blend until smooth. You might need to shake it a few times to get everything to mix. If the mixture is too thick, add a little water, a tablespoon at a time, until you reach your desired consistency.

2 Taste and adjust the seasoning, adding more salt or lemon juice if necessary.

If you want to add hidden veg, add a roasted red pepper or some cooked beetroot to the hummus while blending it. The bonus is a pretty colour!

I sometimes also add a teaspoon or two of harissa for a little kick.

HOMEMADE ROTI

Mauritian roti, often pronounced *rochi*, is a popular traditional flatbread, typically served as a staple with everyday meals. It has a soft, chewy texture and a slightly crispy exterior. Mine always turn out all sorts of shapes because the boys love helping, but the aim is for them to be round! Practice makes perfect, but when you're a mum and have so much to get done, it honestly doesn't matter. Serve these with my Don't Worry Chicken Curry on page 100, or use them in place of soft flour tortillas in any of my recipes.

MAKES 8 LARGE ROTIS

-

500g (1lb 2oz) plain or
    self-raising flour, plus extra
    for dusting
pinch of salt
400–500ml (14–18fl oz) warm
    water
vegetable oil, for frying
butter or ghee, for brushing
    (optional)

Roti is eaten with a variety of accompaniments, such as curry, chutney or even sweet fillings. It's influenced by both Indian and Creole cuisine, reflecting the island's diverse cultural heritage.

1 Combine the flour and a pinch of salt in a large mixing bowl. Gradually add the warm water, a little at a time, mixing with your fingers or a spoon until the dough starts to come together. Add more water or flour if needed – the dough should be pliable but not sticky.

2 Turn it out onto a lightly floured surface and knead for 5–10 minutes until it's smooth and elastic. Place the dough back into the bowl and cover it with a damp cloth. Let it rest for at least 30 minutes.

3 Divide the dough into small balls about the size of a golf ball. Roll out the balls of dough thinly on a lightly floured surface into discs of an even thickness. I tend to roll one out, then fold it a few times and roll it out again.

4 Heat a nonstick frying pan over a medium-high heat. Add 1 teaspoon of vegetable oil and, once hot, place a roti in the pan and cook until you see bubbles forming on the surface (about 30 seconds), then flip it over. Press lightly with a spatula until it puffs up, then flip again and cook for another 10–15 seconds until golden.

5 Remove the cooked roti from the pan and brush with a little butter or ghee for extra flavour and softness if you like. Repeat with the remaining roti and serve warm.

FLUFFY PANCAKE MIX

This is my go-to pancake recipe – they come out fluffy every single time. I use this batter for breakfast pancakes, but also for my Pancake Muffins on page 71. You can also use it to coat, then fry, slices of strawberry and banana, too.

MAKES 6–9

-

200g (7oz) self-raising flour

1½ teaspoons baking powder

2 teaspoons golden caster sugar

pinch of salt

3 eggs

30g (1oz) butter, melted, plus extra for frying

1 teaspoon vanilla extract

200ml (7fl oz) milk

1 Whisk together the flour, baking powder, golden caster sugar and a pinch of salt in a large mixing bowl.

2 In a separate bowl, whisk together the eggs, melted butter and vanilla extract. Add the milk to the egg mixture and combine.

3 Make a well in the centre of the dry ingredients and pour in the wet mixture. Stir gently and mix well until most of the lumps are gone.

4 Heat a nonstick frying pan over a medium heat and add a small knob of butter to grease it. Once the pan is hot, spoon 2–3 tablespoons of the batter into the pan for each pancake. You can use a ladle to help.

5 Cook for 1–2 minutes until bubbles form on the surface, then flip and cook for another 1–2 minutes, until both sides are golden brown. Stack your pancakes and top with your favourite fillings and toppings.

Top or fill your pancakes with fresh fruit, chocolate chips, syrups or sauces, whipped cream or just a light sprinkle of sugar.

GLOSSARY OF UK TO US NAMES

UK NAME	US NAME
baking paper	wax paper/parchment paper
beetroot	beets
caster sugar	superfine sugar
chickpeas	garbanzo beans
coriander (fresh)	cilantro
cornflour	cornstarch
courgette	zucchini
double cream	heavy cream
frying pan	skillet
minced	ground
natural yogurt	plain yogurt
peppers (green/red/yellow)	bell peppers
plain flour	all-purpose flour
roasting tin	roasting pan
spring onions	green onions/scallions
stock	broth
sultanas	golden raisins
sweetcorn	corn
Tenderstem broccoli	broccolini
foil	aluminium foil
tomato purée	tomato paste

INDEX

ACKNOWLEDGMENTS

Creating this cookbook has been a labour of love, and it wouldn't have been possible without the incredible support and inspiration I've received along the way.

To my beautiful boys, Shafi and Kai – you are my biggest inspiration. Watching you grow, eat, explore food and enjoy the little things in life has brought so much joy to my world. You've been Mummy's little helpers and the heart behind these recipes. Thank you for reminding me every day how important it is to embrace happiness and love what you do. I never would have come this far without your unconditional love.

To my fiancé – and the incredibly talented illustrator behind these pages – Tom. You've believed in me, shown me my true worth and been my rock throughout this journey. I couldn't have done any of this without you by my side, cheering me on every step of the way.

Thank you to Octopus Publishing Group. Pauline and Jaz – thank you for believing in my vision. Kate – I'm so grateful you reached out to me; thank you for believing in me. I got really lucky having you all guiding me.

To my family – you were my first taste testers when I started cooking as a young teenager. You're the ones who made food feel like love from the very beginning. Thank you for your patience, your encouragement and for always making me feel like I was onto something special. Your love gave me the confidence to keep ing. And to my friends – your encouragement and ism have meant the world. I don't know how I managed life without all of you.

To my incredible foodie community – your support has been nothing short of amazing. I've connected with so many kind people from around the world, and it still astonishes me how food brings us all together.

To anyone who's ever followed me, tried a recipe from my page, shared or liked a post, or stepped into their kitchen inspired by something I've made – this wouldn't have happened without your love and support. Thank you for trusting me in your kitchens. Your support has meant the world, and I'm constantly amazed by the way food connects us, no matter where we are.

And finally... YOU! I hope this book inspires you to try something new, to cook with love and to make memories around your table with your loved ones. I hope it brings as much joy to your family as it brought to mine in creating it. This book is as much yours as it is mine.

With all my love and gratitude,

Anouska Emily

@emilyscooking_